PHILANTHROPY AND SOCIETY

A comprehensive introduction to the field of philanthropy, *Philanthropy and Society* challenges the reader to think deeply about the role of philanthropic institutions in shaping and bettering the communities they serve and civil society as a whole.

While all agree that the function of philanthropic organizations is to maximize the impact of grant making, there is little consensus on how to do that. This book focuses on two trends that have emerged: strategic philanthropy and increasing diversity, equity and inclusion in philanthropy. Amidst persistent societal inequities, the proliferation of philanthropy leaves one wondering about the potential of this expanding industry to influence social change as well as include constituents beyond donors and their staff. The book offers several case studies of different types of foundations from around the world that demonstrate several tactics used to develop plans that are both strategic and inclusive.

Upper-level undergraduate and postgraduate students of philanthropy, as well as professionals, will come away from this book with a more nuanced and practical sense of the challenging questions the field of philanthropy faces, and the different ways they can be tackled.

David J. Maurrasse, Ph.D., is the Founder & President of Marga Incorporated as well as Research Scholar at the Earth Institute at Columbia University and Adjunct Associate Professor at the School of International and Public Affairs at Columbia University.

"Maurrasse guides the reader through a deep examination of philanthropy, its history, evolution and role in society. He challenges us to answer questions regarding philanthropy's impact, value and relevance; particularly given the demographic shifts in the country as well as the call for diversity, equity and inclusion. We learn through case studies, about the landscape of philanthropy in America and internationally, in the U.K., Africa and global philanthropy efforts by American philanthropy. Ultimately, he elegantly reminds us of philanthropy's responsibility to listen and learn from the communities in which serves, and its inextricable link to the nonprofit sector, if it is to be an agent of change."

Janine Lee, *President and CEO, Southeastern Council of Foundations*

"The issue of inclusive philanthropy is a vital one for funders today, so David Maurrasse's book *Philanthropy and Society* comes at a particularly opportune moment for our field. If funders want to be as effective as possible in reducing the disparities we see today in nearly every aspect of individual and community well-being, it must include the perspectives, voices and participation of the people who are the beneficiaries of their philanthropic efforts. Foundations are always hungry for good examples of how their peers are addressing inclusion in their work, so I'm pleased that this book is centered on foundation case studies. *Philanthropy and Society* is a welcome addition to the body of work on how our field can get better at addressing diversity, equity and inclusion in philanthropy."

David Biemesderfer, *President & CEO, United Philanthropy Forum*

"An expert insider's analysis of how philanthropies are shaping our efforts to make the world a better place and how they can be more inclusive, representative and effective in that quest. The case studies are diverse in every way, compellingly and, taken together, provide a strategy to harness the potential to make doing good better. Makes a strong argument for engagement, place-based solutions, strategic planning, cross-sector partnerships. A GREAT book."

Bill Eimicke, *Professor in the Practice of International and Public Affairs, Columbia University and co-author of* Social Value Investing

PHILANTHROPY AND SOCIETY

David J. Maurrasse

Routledge
Taylor & Francis Group

NEW YORK AND LONDON

First published 2020
by Routledge
52 Vanderbilt Avenue, New York, NY 10017

and by Routledge
2 Park Square, Milton Park, Abingdon, Oxon OX14 4RN

Routledge is an imprint of the Taylor & Francis Group, an informa business

© 2020 Taylor & Francis

Library of Congress Cataloging-in-Publication Data
Names: Maurrasse, David, 1968- author.
Title: Philanthropy and society / David J. Maurrasse.
Description: New York, NY : Routledge, 2020. |
Includes bibliographical references and index.
Identifiers: LCCN 2019047275 | ISBN 9781138731400 (hardback) |
ISBN 9781138731417 (paperback) | ISBN 9781315188997 (ebook)
Subjects: LCSH: Charities. | Charity organization.
Classification: LCC HV25 .M38 2020 | DDC 361.7/4--dc23
LC record available at https://lccn.loc.gov/2019047275

ISBN: 978-1-138-73140-0 (hbk)
ISBN: 978-1-138-73141-7 (pbk)
ISBN: 978-1-315-18899-7 (ebk)

Typeset in Bembo
by Taylor & Francis Books

CONTENTS

FIGURES

ACKNOWLEDGEMENTS

Many at the foundations featured in this book refer to the process of institutional change as a "journey". I can say the same about the process of developing this book. No book project has ever taken me this long. There were many factors at work in lengthening the timing of this effort – some personal and some based on how I designed this process. On the personal side of things, I experienced a life-altering event – the passing of my mother in the summer of 2017. As an unmarried, childless person, I had never really broken a deep bond with my mother into adulthood. So, this occurrence rattled me unlike any other experience. I had originally expected to complete this project around late 2017 or early 2018. I certainly appreciate the patience Taylor & Francis/Routledge demonstrated with my multiple extension requests over the last few years.

As my mother was such a consistent presence in my life, I dedicate this book to her posthumously. This isn't the first time I have dedicated a book to her. But it is only fitting in that I am not sure what I would be or where I would be without the 49 years of my life that I fortunately got to spend with her. Furthermore, if philanthropy is the love of humanity, it is also appropriate that I dedicate this book to the memory of my mother, Daphne Agatha Maurrasse. If there were ever a person in my life capable of putting the needs of others beyond her own, it was my mother. She watched over so many people she encountered over the course of her life, who were scattered in various parts of the world. We can only hope that the field of philanthropy can live up to the unselfish values of those like my mother well into the future.

Another reason this book project extended over the course of a few years was my chosen method to seek approval from the foundations featured herein for their participation in the research. Not only did they agree to be investigated, they saw the chapters in which they were featured. I want to thank the Mary

Reynolds Babcock Foundation, the San Francisco Foundation, the LankellyChase Foundation, TrustAfrica, the Conrad Hilton Foundation, and the Meyer Memorial Trust for their participation in this project. These foundations were selected because they had a story to tell about how they engage their constituents and bring their ideas into the foundation's thinking and practice.

I certainly realize that some might dismiss this book immediately, because the featured foundations got to approve their chapters. This book is not uncritical of foundations and philanthropy. I am very aware of the many critiques of philanthropy circulating at this time. I would say that the foundations in this book, to varying degrees, are working through their own questions about the value and purpose of philanthropy. The idea for this book was driven by a genuine desire to imagine philanthropy's responsibility to society in action. There is no mandate telling foundations exactly how they should give, and certainly not one challenging them to make sure they partner with the communities their grants might impact before deciding how to proceed. In identifying foundations to feature, I was looking for institutions that want to rise to the occasion, strengthen lines of communications with communities, and be willing to change based on what they hear from external constituents with lived experiences in the issue areas that so many foundations seek to address.

Thanks to the New World Foundation, and Colin Greer in particular. Colin and the New World Foundation supported this project from the very beginning substantively and financially. I have known Colin for many years now. He is a true veteran in philanthropy, who has always brought incredible insights and creativity to the New World Foundation and the philanthropic field, as is demonstrated in his foreword for this book.

The institutional research home for this book, and most of my research in recent years, is the Earth Institute at Columbia University. The Earth Institute is where my research line at Columbia University resides. The Institute houses the funding to support the research as well as the many research assistants who have worked with me on this project across several semesters now. Special thanks to Hayley Martinez at the Earth Institute, who has been administering grants management and human resources for this effort. Thanks to research assistants, including Alison Kelman, Sophia Grace Davis, and Michele Favero.

Franck Gbaguidi identified TrustAfrica as a prospect for this book, and interviewed various stakeholders from this foundation. This was a notable load for a research assistant to carry for which I am grateful. Franck was among a cluster of research assistants who worked together at an earlier stage in this process, which also included Joey DeMarco, Angie Goenaga, and Stephanie Hoyt. I appreciate the work this particular cluster of researchers conducted, as they contributed at an early stage when the challenge was to find foundations that would be a fit for this project, which would also be willing to be investigated.

At this stage in my life, my main professional hat is at Marga Incorporated, the company I founded. Staff at Marga tend to get drawn into my research and writing projects. One person in particular, Shangchao Liu played a significant role in developing many aspects of this book. I want to thank Shangchao for his incredible dedication and consistency. I would also like to thank Erica Chung, who played an instrumental role in drafting and organizing the chapter on Trus-tAfrica, as well as reviewing other chapters. Thanks as well to Cynthia C. Jones for consistent support over many years.

The work of Marga Incorporated has put me in touch with some extraordinary leaders in philanthropy who have been challenging this field to be responsive to communities, and to be diverse, equitable, and inclusive. People such as Susan Batten of the Association of Black Foundation Executives, Janine Lee of the Southeastern Council on Foundations, Darren Walker of the Ford Foundation, Chet Hewitt of the Sierra Health Foundation are among those I have known for over two decades, who have maintained a healthy balance between recognizing philanthropy's promise, and challenging its limitations. There are many, many others whom I have encountered over the years in philanthropy, who have shaped my thinking about what's possible when we raise our expectations about philanthropy's responsibility to society. Also, Marga has had the privilege of coordinating the efforts of the Race and Equity in Philanthropy Group, and working with numerous foundations and philanthropy serving organizations (PSOs) over the years. I would not have even thought to write this book without these experiences. For this, I am very appreciative.

As in any book project, there are many others to thank beyond those who are named here. I want to appreciate everyone who touched any aspect of putting this book together from the beginning to the end. And, finally, I would like to recognize the communities in which the featured foundations are working. The residents and organizations in these communities had a profound effect on the strategic priorities of these six foundations. They brought society into philanthropy, enabling these foundations to, at the very least, be more responsive to the communities they hope to impact.

FOREWORD

By Colin Greer, President, New World Foundation

David has chosen his cases well and revealed them in an exemplary instructive fashion. So, we can take assurance that leading foundations and their leaders have broken the back of some historic conventions that inhibit social change. These remarks will address those considerations in the practice of effective philanthropy.

In the first part of this short essay I address the way in which foundations can adapt their practice to listen for and adapt to understanding of the field and people they do or might support.

In the second I consider the imperative to transform the non-democratic sources of the accumulation of foundation assets into more democratic ways of relating to the greater world and of understanding how democracy can be either undermined (even with topical success) or enlivened by foundation insight and reform.

In the already changing picture of foundation practice the following practices stand out:

1. Time limited funding makes way for multi-year. In the past, reflex practices cut off grantees after three or five years no matter what. Long term involvement in making change has rarely been at the heart of social practice. Nowadays, it is more likely that strong initiative can be given the time to educate a public, build policy options, practice living in a changed environment.

2. Project funding which limits creative adaptation is being displaced by general support grantmaking. Now we understand that non-profit service and advocacy organization have to build and support an infrastructure that

makes project effectiveness possible. If not, then disappointment follows, leaders are discredited and organizations are weakened.

3. Site visits are much more likely now than ever, i.e. actually engaging grantees in situ. This promotes foundation staff's understanding and sets up the possibility for relationship building leading to actual information and analysis. As a corollary to that foundations bring a wider view to the field (e.g. policy, social, and economic umbrella conditions, geopolitical fallout, etc.)

4. Leverage is important. More often, foundations recognize that if the work they fund is to be of significance they should use their leverage to bring in additional resources. This allows previously underfunded projects to reach scale or raise the "follow through" money that can take promising work to demonstrable success. Using that leverage is now much more acceptable, and not seen as special pleading.

5. Grantees on foundation boards was once the exclusive preserve of families and their closest peers in shared social milieu. More foundations than ever have added grantees to their boards recognizing that having ears to the ground in discussion and strategic design is of great value.

6. Foundation staff come from the field of practice and study. (Nowadays foundations recruit some staff from practice, even from amongst the most humble, least credentialed, they recognize that experience and intellect matter and their having been nurtured in the work arena (geographic or demographic) improves chances of sound grantmaking choices.

All these changes allow for community well-being to serve as an umbrella strategic goal in the pursuit of particular ends.

At this point I'd like to emphasize that philanthropy is an instrument of public policy. Though it is often considered a private domain, it is not. The tax codes enshrine a delicate balance between devolution of inequity, discovery, and invention for public good. Money that could otherwise be collected in taxes is assigned to charitable purposes—it is a public policy choice administered through private analysis and distribution.

Too often the sense of entitled private ownership has promoted whimsical giving, short attention span, and private interests (even good ones) determined by personal situations and faulty interests.

When all this transpires as it frequently does then the delicate balance is thrown off. Just as in Part I above I described practices that constitute a voluntary evolution of philanthropy to improve its effectiveness and remake the state of the art of giving, so here I am proposing a reform agenda – voluntarily adopted – to rectify the imbalance in favor of greater democratic awareness and operations. Indeed, I have yet a further gain in mind: namely, the role of philanthropy in revivifying democratic life in America by modeling and teaching democratic practices.

A Reform Agenda

1. Refrain from naming opportunities. Why create monuments to individual persons or organizations when the money is held in public trust? Anonymous can stand for public policy delivered.

2. Adopt a philanthropic sector property tax to allow endowed institutions to continue to benefit from discounted tax but not deprive communities of local taxes when large institutions occupy large tracts of land or build offices on sought after urban setting, the zero property tax exemption afforded them diminishes local resources considerably, at times disastrously. Indeed, a sector property tax could apply to any non-profit institution that does not provide direct services (that is: do not provide food, health care, counselling, shelter) to the most needy and are of a size that taxes are meaningful.

3. Forgo the sales tax forgiveness benefit. Why should endowments (Gates, Ford, Harvard, etc.,) not pay tax on their computers, stationery, and so many other purchases? While endowments grow ever larger in the US the cost to the neighboring communities (in the loss of local and federal taxes) is monumental. At the same time while foundations' required payout includes administrative costs, it is not restricted to grantmaking. The expenditures requirements (5% in the US) includes the costs of overhead, as well as grantmaking. This means that sales tax forgiveness creates a double benefit for the same dollar expenditure.

4. Or, following up on #3: assign only actual grantmaking to the payout requirement. Assign the costs to the business of infrastructure necessary to general operations. Simply add this to the cost of overhead separated from payout.

5. Wealth carries great authority. In a time when corporate solutions seem, to many, to be superior to public efforts, wealth has taken on a pseudo sacred caste. To illuminate and legitimate democratically formed governments and their responsibility to serve the public interest at the national, regional, and local level it is critical that all grantees and all public information systems are clear that philanthropy is a public (government) created and charged sector, an estate of the Republic as are the press, religious institutions, and other non-governmental institutions.

6. Convene an Accreditation Authority, much as Universities engage in peer review and/or are approved by state authorities. Why not have foundations declare purpose and assess their effectiveness every five years. This will establish a peer learning environment, a public record, and a more transparent style.

7. We live in a time without a clear set of restraints on global capitalism and its super-corporate hold on public policy and leaders. But a map is being drawn by base-building activist organizations, as well as think-tank and advocacy groups. Of these, the base-building organizations are the root from which

movements for social justice and equity grow. At the heart of any such
movement are the people who suffer injustice, who organize to oppose it,
and who build organizations that transform victims into empowered agents.
When successful, such movements can produce extraordinary leaps of progress, even in the most daunting times.

It is such groups that we at New World Foundation (NWF) embrace in our
grantmaking. These organizations in communities nationwide are often despe-
rately short of resources. In a recent survey, we found that among more than 50
base-building activist organizations (some of the strongest in the field by our
lights) close to 90 percent were dependent on limited foundation support, with
minimal sources of other tax-exempt money, and many of their executive
directors and senior staff lived very close to the poverty line.

NWF has gradually, over the past 20 years, established these executive directors
and their organizations as the major partners in the work we share. A series of
basic principles defines our approach to becoming a reliable and trusted partner of
such social justice organizations. I present those principles as time (30 years) tested
approaches that have proved effective and meaningful to all concerned.

- *Accountability to social justice activists / Building grantee participation into the decision-
  making of the Foundation*
- We have taken seriously the proposition that we must aim to be the change
  we seek and that this is as important a goal for the Foundation as for its
  grantees. To do that, we have chosen to be accountable to those we fund,
  recognizing that such accountability is our choice, since there are few legal
  requirements for philanthropic accountability. We have, over time, moved
  our board from family and friends of an original donor to a board made up
  mostly of people of color and individuals who have been, are, or might be
  grantees of the Foundation. This board both gives the Foundation legitimacy
  in the field and ensures that its decision-making includes the experience of
  work on the ground.
- *Sharing risk with grantees*
- Social justice activists work in organizations that are, for the most part, des-
  perately underfunded, with a chronically overworked senior staff. The risk of
  burnout is ever present and every budget year brings the risk of shrinkage.
  The Foundation has tried to share that risk by maintaining a high payout
  level, usually twice the required legal minimum. We do not operate on the
  principle that our long-term survival is the most significant consideration in
  the use of our resources.
- *Finding a balance between assessment and partnership through reciprocal responsibility*
- We aim, not always successfully, for reliable and respectful communication
  with grantees, demanding of ourselves speedy, clear and supportive standards
  when asking grantees for information or responding to their requests for

information and help from us. NWF supports organizations for the long haul, no "three years and you're out". We fund only with general support grants, not project grants, and we encourage and support collaborations among grantees, trying to limit competition for resources and maximize solidarity. We commit our staff to supporting the fundraising efforts of grantees from colleagues with whom we have closer relationships, so that we add a powerful resource to the financial development of social justice organizations. Criteria for evaluation are jointly devised by our field staff and our partners/grantees. The consequent strength of these relationships is crucial to the assessment of effectiveness and the development of strategy. We do not select on the basis of written proposals, and we do not judge on the basis of written reports. We aim to be colleagues, and we demand from our grantees leadership and democratic participation in respect of both their organization and our continuing work.

- *Stability in the organizational life of grantees who are dependent on foundations*
- We've learned that social justice leaders often work close to the edge of poverty, as well as to the edge of exhaustion. While we can't make a great difference to the overall level of compensation in the field, what we can do is create space for spiritual and physical recovery and opportunities for intellectual re-engagement with theory, history and networking by providing sabbatical awards. The Alston/Bannerman awards, which both provide respite and encourage the development of secondary leadership, are given by a panel, the great majority of whom are former fellows of the program. This helps build mutual respect, confirms the value of each other's work, and offers opportunities to become part of long-term movement building, as a counterpoint to the day-to-day grind of the work. We encourage and support cross-sectoral partnerships between social justice CBOs and human service professionals and those working in the political arena. Our goal is to limit competition and maximize cooperation and solidarity among social justice activists, and to advance social justice expectations in a wider public.

Does any of this mean we are never high-handed? That we make decisions our grantee allies always cheer? No, it doesn't. But it does mean that we, and a few solid colleague foundations, have begun to establish an order of criteria and practice, which recognizes the need for foundations supporting social justice work to, just like their grantees, grow into social justice organizations themselves.

INTRODUCTION

In various ways, philanthropy has become increasingly central in our lives. We hear stories of extremely wealthy individuals making giving pledges. Manifestations of philanthropy are numerous and more varied than ever. Notions of investment once exclusive to the banking industry, have found their way into philanthropy, along with other ideas common to the world of business. Additionally, charitable giving is weaved into the fabric of life at all levels. When there is a natural disaster, people find ways to chip in. Communities from all backgrounds demonstrate forms of philanthropy that may not resemble the practices of the wealthy and foundations. But people in communities help each other. They may not give money to incorporated organizations, but they find ways to support others' ability to make ends meet. People barter. People share.

But what is the purpose of philanthropy? Is it merely the extension of those who want to do good in some capacity? Is it a way for those of means to immortalize themselves? To whom are philanthropists accountable? And what of the intended beneficiaries of philanthropy – the hungry, the sick, the impoverished – those who many philanthropists say they want to help? What is their role? After over a century of the development of modern philanthropy, many are questioning some fundamental and traditional assumptions about this concept and the myriad institutions that have been established around it.

Philanthropy has evolved through the ages. The earliest forms of philanthropy date back to the 10th century with Sung Dynasty philanthropists funding the creation of poor houses, soup kitchens and orphanages.[1] The origins of philanthropy in the United States were influenced strongly by religious beliefs and traditions, communal practices of Native American communities, and support within immigrant and settler communities.[2] Religious organizations predominantly spearheaded philanthropic efforts centered on almsgiving and volunteering.[3]

This form of philanthropy continued until Andrew Carnegie's Gospel of Wealth spurred a new movement of millionaires to utilize their wealth for the public good in less traditional areas, thus catalyzing profound effects on education, culture, science and public health.[4] This process naturally resulted in a more systematic approach to philanthropy in solving social issues.[5] The end of World War II saw the professionalization of philanthropic institutions in support of civil and human rights and minority causes, often led by women.[6] This period also gave rise to an expansion of community foundations. Combining scientific philanthropy, grantmaking foundations and collective giving; this new type of foundation changed the definition of who could give – not just the wealthy, but also individuals of all other socioeconomic statuses.[7] Philanthropy now is more organized and professional than ever and has taken on a role where individuals can donate to champion a variety of different causes, but also one where technology and cutting-edge research fuel local and global projects.[8] As of 2015, there were over 86,203 grantmaking foundations in the U.S.[9], and foundation giving in 2018 increased to $75.86 billion, which is a 7.3% increase from 2017.[10]

The dictionary definition of philanthropy (goodwill to fellow members of the human race)[11] is so broad that it does not fully illustrate the actual contemporary manifestation of the idea. In reality, most experience philanthropy as the distribution of financial resources to support various services and other initiatives pursued by nonprofit/nongovernmental organizations. An identifiable philanthropic field has gradually emerged, especially in North America and Europe. Within this field, dialogue has begun to grow around the roles and responsibilities of donors and philanthropic institutions. External to this field, questions have surfaced as well. Some have demanded greater accountability and transparency in foundations. Others have advocated for improved impact and demonstrable results. Some others have suggested philanthropy open up and deepen connections to the communities it serves. All of these perspectives have influenced the emergence of different approaches to how foundations distribute resources to increase impact and accountability. These ideas are driven by varying motivations. This book is ultimately interested in the ability of foundations to stretch their ability to reduce inequities by way of strategic approaches to giving, which are also inclusive. How do foundations engage and include their constituents in shaping their strategic priorities?

This inquiry emerges out of two significant trends that have surfaced out of desires to improve philanthropy's impact, value, and relevance. One of these trends is the concept of strategic philanthropy, which promotes focused programming, especially among philanthropic institutions (foundations) in various substantive areas (i.e. literacy) designed to achieve demonstrable and measurable results. Another is a growing call to increase diversity, equity, and inclusion (DEI) in philanthropy. A subset of dialogue around DEI has more directly highlighted racial equity.

These suggestions point to the concentration of power and control in foundation policies, practices, and programs among homogenous, dominant populations. Critiques of philanthropy's lack of diversity, equity, and inclusion raise questions about strategic philanthropy. As strategy formulation typically rests with high level executives, the role and involvement of broader and more diverse constituents in shaping and implementing strategies is an important consideration. In 2018 racial and ethnic minorities only comprised 9.7 percent of CEOs, while the ratio of minorities in total professional positions including CEO, Associate Director and Vice President was about 32.8 percent.[12] If wealthy philanthropists and high-level executives (who are not especially diverse), typically set strategic priorities, can resulting strategies realistically meet the needs of ultimate intended beneficiary populations?

If a foundation intends to promote preventative health measures in low income communities of color, how can it effectively design and implement such a strategy without substantial input from those populations? Often health disparities correlate very strongly with race and ethnicity as well as socioeconomic class.[13] Therefore, the notion of greater DEI in philanthropy has a functional and strategic dimension. The mission of most philanthropic initiatives would be enhanced with greater inclusion of intended beneficiary populations. A health foundation would likely be better positioned to reduce health inequities with an intimate connection with those most adversely impacted in their health outcomes.

Another emerging conversation in philanthropy focuses on power dynamics. The National Committee for Responsive Philanthropy (NCRP) has spearheaded this conversation by continually pushing for foundations to fund projects for the marginalized, underserved and disenfranchised.[14] Foundations and philanthropists occupy a unique position in the nonprofit sector, which places the majority of nonprofit organizations beneath philanthropy; a dynamic in which funders and those seeking grants or donations are on opposite sides. The world of philanthropy becomes insulated from the broader nonprofit sector in this scenario. Relationships between nonprofits and foundations or donors can potentially become entirely transactional in this instance. Inclusion is crucial in helping us navigate how to mitigate potentially negative effects of power dynamics because it places the intended beneficiary populations and more diverse populations in decision-making or, at the very least, influence. While those with the money are legally entitled to spend it based on the wishes of donors or foundation staff, who should play a role in shaping the direction of grants and donations in various specific fields of interest?

This book is particularly concerned with the concept of inclusion, and the degree to which the development and execution of philanthropic strategy includes broader constituents. These constituents could be representatives of intended beneficiary populations, potential partners, or diverse constituents that may not be among grantee populations. Inclusion is similar to, but distinct from, diversity. Diversity in itself is quantitative – changing the numbers of demographics. Inclusion connotes active participation among constituents. Inclusion is manifested in various forms, such as the composition of foundations' Boards and executive staff, involvement in committees, advisory groups, or focus groups that inform foundations' practice, routine lines of communication with grantee communities, and other formats that facilitate how strategies, policies, and practices are designed, unveiled, and implemented. The key point with inclusion is that those who are brought into these formats are influential, where constituent voices are welcomed and actually employed in decision making.

One example of an approach to include the voices of ultimate beneficiary populations was developed by a network of foundations – The Fund for Shared Insight. This Fund has been promoting feedback loops designed to reach populations that are typically the "least heard". Their methodology, *Listen for Good* (L4G) encourages foundations to build and maintain ongoing feedback loops to hear from beneficiary populations. The Fund is specific about their target population. It is not nonprofit organizations that receive grants. These are "intermediaries" according to the Fund. They are interested in increasing how foundations include the perspectives and wisdom of the populations served by the nonprofits. Consequently, they are not focused on the executive leading the homeless shelter, they are interested in hearing from the homeless themselves.[15] Feedback loops are important. The Fund has developed a useful tool. Some other foundations are trying different ways to be simultaneously inclusive and strategic. Once one recognizes the strategic value of inclusion, techniques to ensure inclusion can vary. What can be learned from such approaches that are both strategic and inclusive? And what role can these methods play in reducing the concentration of power in philanthropy, and increasing foundations' impact regarding the various social and economic concerns that a considerable portion of philanthropy seeks to address?

Private philanthropy, which has set aside private capital for the maintenance and/or perpetuity of foundations and the distribution of charitable gifts, has grown into an industry of hundreds of billions of dollars in the United States. Philanthropy has expanded around the world as well, not only in Europe, but in Asia, the Middle East, Latin America, and elsewhere. And some globally oriented philanthropic institutions (i.e. the Bill and Melinda Gates Foundation) include grantmaking around the world, particularly in developing nations. Amidst persistent societal inequities and various other challenges in society, the proliferation of philanthropy leaves one wondering about the potential of this expanding industry to truly influence social change as well as include constituents beyond donors and their staff.

Discussions of philanthropy have been addressing the industry's promise and pitfalls via numerous angles. Do foundations properly recognize the realities of the administrative costs of nonprofit organizations? Are foundation dollars too short term and restrictive? Does philanthropy impose too many expectations and evaluations to enable grant recipients to do their work effectively? Can foundations become more catalytic in how they make their gifts or "investments"? How can these dollars effectively complement resources from the public sector and other foundations? Can models that merge profits with social gain through "impact investing" truly increase the value and influence of philanthropic dollars? The answers to these questions are continually addressed by philanthropic professionals. But the nature of these answers is informed by who is responsible for grappling with the questions. Underlying some of the critiques of philanthropy is the suggestion that philanthropy is out of touch with the reality of community-based nonprofit organizations and lower income communities. If philanthropic solutions are not informed by broader populations, how can they succeed? And some wonder whether philanthropy intends to bring about social change at all given that the field's capital is controlled by those who do not stand to gain from any major social and economic upheaval.

Considerations about the potential of philanthropy are plentiful. Increasingly, philanthropists and observers alike promote various forms of "strategic" philanthropy. Whereas an individual or institutional donor could make singular gifts to different causes without a particular theme or connection across a series of contributions, a strategic approach would be a more intentional endeavor. A foundation could, for example, identify three major issues in which it hopes to make a substantial impact, and carefully select a few grantees to carry out an agenda over a period of several years. In the more professionalized segments in the philanthropic field, such as the foundations participating in the Council on Foundations, this is certainly the trend.

Foundations come in multiple forms, all of which strive to be as strategic and/ or impactful as possible in their methods. Increasingly, foundations are confronted with how to become more inclusive. This is partly due to changing demographics, external pressure, and other variables. Some foundation structures might be more equipped to encompass the voices of multiple constituents in their design and implementation than others. Community foundations, which pool the resources of multiple donors with an emphasis on a specific geographical area, can construct multiple formats for giving by and for different constituents through funds and giving circles.

Community foundations are continually evolving, and proliferating in regions large and small, urban and rural. These types of foundations are often an avenue to grants for smaller localized nonprofit organizations. And as the nonprofit sector continues to expand throughout the U.S. and elsewhere, so does the need for philanthropic dollars. Community foundations are also highly donor driven, with their array of donor advised funds and giving circles, which are focused philanthropic pursuits directly informed by the interests of donors who established accounts at a community foundation. This culture of donor intent, while potentially inclusive, is often manifested exclusively.

Corporate foundations, which are nonprofit organizations spun off and informed by for profit corporations have become avenues to express the social values of large corporations, and even further their business operations. And, various other forms of foundations, such as health conversion foundations, which are established out of the remaining assets of dissolved health care institutions, are providing new structures and approaches to philanthropic giving. These structures are typically created with Boards of Directors representative of the communities these foundations ultimately serve; whereas the strategies of corporate foundations are often driven by the priorities of their parent companies.

Philanthropy as we know it today has evolved substantially from the original pursuits of the wealthy of prior generations, such as John D. Rockefeller or Andrew Carnegie, who developed institutions that have existed in perpetuity due to enduring endowments. Some living philanthropists, such as George Soros, have created philanthropic institutions that are designed to spend down their assets rather than hold on to them, while giving away small increments each year. Spending down is a strategy in itself that is poised to expend larger amounts in shorter periods of time. Newer wealthy philanthropists are increasingly making contributions with the intent to spend the vast majority of their philanthropic capital in their lifetimes. And many of these donors are bringing a business orientation to their giving, focusing heavily on results. These perspectives have helped encourage a greater emphasis on strategy in philanthropy.

With this growing and multifaceted philanthropic landscape, what does this mean for society and the intended beneficiaries of these contributions? Indeed, this is a general and central question confronting the entire field. But it is an important query to pose with respect to philanthropy's capacity to incorporate broader and more diverse constituents into their policies, practices, and programmatic strategies.

Indeed, popular conceptions of philanthropy emphasize the wealthy. Foundations and other forms of charitable giving are often viewed as extensions of the wealthy. However, one does not have to be wealthy to be philanthropic. Lower income communities have been helping each other philanthropically for generations. Many people of all economic levels make contributions to nonprofit organizations in some capacity. Tithing in religious institutions has existed for centuries. We have witnessed an expansion and transformation of philanthropy, which exists alongside conceptions of the role of government as well as the decreasing influence and resources of government. In many instances, government alone does not have the capacity to meet the needs of populations.

As civil society can be represented by the nonprofit sector, philanthropy can bring the capital that facilitates the practices of nonprofit organizations. Ideally, this is the framework of a functional role for philanthropy in civil society, especially in democracies. But is this really the case? In the midst of philanthropic growth, are we seeing an expanded voice of civil society or even a reduction in the inequities that many philanthropic institutions purport to address? If philanthropic strategy is going to lead to reduced inequities, to what degree can greater inclusion of broader constituencies (especially intended beneficiary populations) influence impact?

Considerations regarding strategy and inclusion in philanthropy are relevant beyond U.S. boundaries. How philanthropy can integrate the perspectives and involvement of broader constituents in shaping and implementing strategies is a universal concept. It is relevant for the quality and effectiveness of philanthropic initiatives. The international development community, for example, has increasingly recognized the significance of securing buy-in from recipient communities in developing countries so that interventions are not merely outside efforts based on external expert opinions. And some global foundations have intentionally established satellite offices led by representatives of local constituents.

Inclusive strategies are not perfect. And inclusion is not an automatic pathway to the most effective and impactful strategies. But they challenge some aspects of power in philanthropy and potentially help craft solutions to some of the most seemingly intractable social and economic concerns. It is difficult to adequately reduce inequities when the communities that are disproportionately impoverished and marginalized are not informing the strategies ostensibly for their benefit. And no singular foundation, even with tens of billions, can sufficiently solve any significant problem even with a single-issue focus. Consequently, some dimension of partnership with institutions beyond singular foundations is an important aspect of strategic inclusion as well.

Philanthropic efforts that are both strategic and inclusive continue to emerge and evolve. This book explores six case examples of philanthropic strategies that prioritize inclusion in the U.S. and elsewhere. In each of these six case studies, this book outlines a foundation's strategy, examines how the foundation developed an inclusive strategic approach, assesses the strengths and challenges of the approach, and analyzes the approach's impact and long-term viability. These cases have been informed by interviews with foundation officials and relevant constituents, and online research.

The next chapter includes an overview of the landscape of contemporary philanthropy, including discussion of some relevant trends, such as the emergence of strategic philanthropy and the growing effort to improve diversity, equity, and inclusion in the field. The bulk of the book includes profiles that capture the ideas and techniques of foundations attempting to complement their philanthropic strategy development with an increased emphasis on inclusion. These six chapters provide case examples, including the approaches of various types of foundations across the United States and in different national contexts. The remainder of the book analyzes lessons drawn from the examples and recommends some new directions for philanthropy informed by the experiences of profiled foundations.

The first profiled foundation represents a U.S.-based private foundation's effort to incorporate an explicit commitment to inclusion in its philanthropic strategy with a particular emphasis on equity. The second case example focuses on a foundation in the developed world, but not in the U.S., which has deeply connected with constituents in various localities in its region. The third case features a community foundation that is pursuing an especially inclusive strategy stressing equity among multiple demographic groups in its target geographical area. The fourth profile explores how a globally oriented U.S.-based large private foundation, working in an African nation, has emphasized inclusive partnerships to expand community-based participation in shaping programming. The fifth case example focuses on a U.S.-based family foundation aiming to increase impact through a strategically inclusive approach. The final case profiles a homegrown African philanthropic initiative, which was created in order to develop strategies that are by and for Africans, reflecting the perspectives and interests of local communities across the continent.

The remainder of the book reflects upon lessons learned from the experiences of these different types of foundation, draws conclusions and offer recommendations. As philanthropy is a multifaceted field, there is no single perfect way to make foundations and donors more responsive to society. However, the intent of this book is to highlight examples of different approaches that varying types of foundations are pursuing to strengthen how the voices of constituent populations shape their priorities.

Notes

1 (National-Philanthropic-Trust 2018)
2 (Philanthropy New York 2017)
3 (Philanthropy New York 2017)
4 (National-Philanthropic-Trust 2018)
5 (Philanthropy New York 2017)
6 (National-Philanthropic-Trust 2018)
7 (Philanthropy New York 2017)
8 (National-Philanthropic-Trust 2018)
9 (Foundation Center 2015)
10 (Giving USA 2019)
11 (Merriam-Webster 2018)
12 (Council on Foundations 2018)
13 (Barr 2008)
14 (National Committee for Responsive Philanthropy 2018)
15 (Fund for Shared Insight 2014)

References

Barr, Donald A. *Health Disparities in the United States.* Baltimore: Johns Hopkins University Press, 2008.
Council on Foundations. *Grantmaker Salary and Benefits Report.* 2018. https://www.ctp hilanthropy.org/sites/default/files/resources/2018%20Grantmaker%20Salary%20and% 20Benefits%20Report.pdf.

Foundation Center. *Key Facts on U.S. Foundations*. 2015.

Fund for Shared Insight. *Fund for Shared Insight*. 2014. https://www.fundforsharedinsight. org/ (accessed September 24, 2018).

Giving USA. "Giving USA 2019." 2019.

Merriam-Webster. *Definition of Philanthropy*. https://www.merriam-webster.com/dictionary/ philanthropy.

National Committee for Responsive Philanthropy. *About NCRP: Our Mission*. 2018. https:// www.ncrp.org/about-us (accessed September 24, 2018).

National-Philanthropic-Trust. *A History of Modern Philanthropy*. 2018. http://www.historyofgiv ing.org/1500-1750/1600-philanthropy-enters-the-english-language/ (accessed September 23, 2018).

Philanthropy New York. *History of U.S. Philanthropy*. 2017. https://philanthropynewyork. org/ (accessed October 4, 2018).

1

THE STATE OF PHILANTHROPY

The Current Landscape of Philanthropy

Philanthropy continues to grow in the United States and in many other nations. The number of foundations continues to proliferate. The range of forms of private giving is becoming increasingly extensive. Overall, private philanthropy is becoming more integrated into our lives. For example, in the wake of natural disasters, it has become commonplace for individuals to make private contributions toward recovery. In parts of the world where philanthropy was not central even a decade ago, policies are being instituted to provide incentives (i.e. tax deductions) for private giving. Increasingly, we are witnessing growing expectations that private giving supplement government shortfalls on issues such as education. We have even seen private philanthropy bail out local governments.[1]

Philanthropy is not a replacement for government. Typically, the levels of giving that private philanthropy can support fall far short of the cost of running public systems and programs. The advantage of private philanthropic money is flexibility. While many foundation grants are restricted, the nature of work that private philanthropic dollars can support (i.e. planning) is fairly broad. These private resources might not be able to solve major intractable societal challenges on their own, but they can complement government programs and stimulate innovation. Philanthropic dollars can do great things – creating vaccinations, building schools, stimulating job growth. This is part of the appeal of philanthropy and the nonprofit sector – the ability to do good with a sense of entrepreneurship. There is always a problem that needs solving and a need for new ways to address this issue. Some would say we have too many nonprofit organizations because of this spirit.

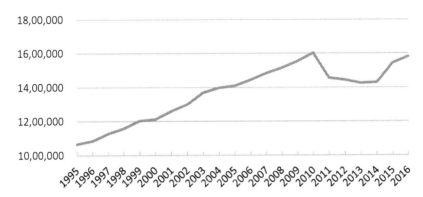

FIGURE 1.1 Number of Registered Nonprofit Organizations in the U.S.
Source: National Center for Charitable Statistics 2016

The definitive number of nonprofit organizations worldwide is not available due to the absence of an international repository of comprehensive statistics. But the fact remains that in almost every country the nonprofit sector has been growing rapidly in terms of the total number of nonprofit organizations.[2] As Figure 1.1 depicts, despite the sharp drop in the early years of the 2010s, the total number of registered nonprofit organizations in the U.S. has increased by 48.2% from 1,066,804 in 1995 to 1,581,445 in 2016. Similar trends have been found in many other countries such as India, South Korea, Spain, Saudi Arabia, etc.[3]

According to the categorization of nonprofit organization in the U.S., there are three types of nonprofit organizations: private foundations, public charities, and other nonprofit organizations. We can also see growth in the number of private foundations. Figure 1.2 shows that in the U.S., the number of registered private foundations has increased from 518,182 in 1995 to 1,108,652 in 2016. Globally, the exact total number of private foundations is not available, but its growing

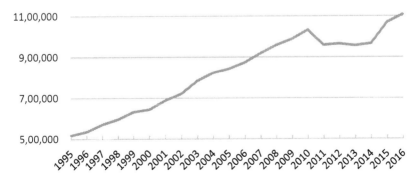

FIGURE 1.2 Number of Registered Private Foundations in the U.S.
Source: National Center for Charitable Statistics 2016

trend is observable.[4] As indicated in the *Global Philanthropy Report*, [5] 260,358 foundations in 38 countries and Hong Kong are identified, but this is only part of the global picture. The report also points out that "the number of philanthropic institutions has skyrocketed in this century".

Despite the accomplishments of philanthropy to date, foundation dollars could do so much more. The inclusion of perspectives from intended beneficiary populations in strategy development could be an important pathway to helping maximize foundations' resources.

Broader Trends in the Field

The growth in philanthropy is an overarching trend affecting the field. Whenever a field experiences this level of growth, professional infrastructure follows. In the United States, the philanthropic field, particularly with respect to institutional philanthropy (as opposed to individuals and small families) has evolved. The Council on Foundations has been the central professional association for institutional philanthropy. But the landscape of associations representing subsets within philanthropy has widened as well, including associations for particular geographical areas (known as Regional Associations of Grantmakers), associations for particular population groups, and associations focused on specific issue areas. These various associations have come to be known as Philanthropy Serving Organizations (PSOs). The United Philanthropy Forum is the association, which brings all of these PSOs together.

Beyond the United States, associations focused on philanthropy have been created as well. In various countries, national governments coordinate how foundations come together. For example, in the United Kingdom, the Association of Charitable Foundations (ACF), a membership body for UK foundations and grant-making charities, was founded in 1989 to support the operation and coordination of charities via providing advocacy, information, a program of events, and a variety of other services. ACF has been privatized to a charitable company limited since 2005. In China, foundations are registered, regulated, and monitored by the Chinese Ministry of Civil Affairs; however, the information and advocacy services at the national level is mainly provided by a few public charities such as the China Foundation Center (CFC).

As philanthropy often starts with the individual, some donors are foregoing creating new institutions designed to be endowed and to exist in perpetuity. They are focusing on social investments and/or donor advised funds (DAFs). According to the 2017 Donor-Advised Fund report by the National Philanthropic Trust,[6] the number of individual donor-advised funds has grown steadily since 2012 with an average annual growth rate of 6%. In 2016, there were 284,965 donor-advised funds in the U.S. In addition, contributions to donor-advised funds totaled an unprecedented US$23.27 billion; grants from donor-advised funds also exceeded $15 billion in 2016, with a compound annual growth rate of 18.8% since 2012.

Community foundations have grown because of DAFs. The appeal is the opportunity to allow another institution to handle administration, while the donor can recommend contributions from the fund. Community foundations typically offer services for donors with DAFs that can help guide their giving.

Foundations have continually been confronted with how to increase their impact and effectively measure progress. In many ways, this concern gave rise to an emphasis on strategic philanthropy. Greater attention to evaluation and assessment remains an important trend. Strategic philanthropy is related due to its intent to sharpen focus, clarify goals, and develop indicators reflective of goals. Many foundations were scrutinized for a lack of focus – merely giving grants without any guiding themes.

Policies significantly influence the composition of philanthropy. For instance, changes to tax laws or policies could significantly affect philanthropic activities. Charitable tax deductions are significant incentives for philanthropic giving. If the income tax rate is lower, charitable giving could be expected to decrease due to the less significant scale of tax deduction. Similarly, the proposed elimination or reduction of estate taxes could be beneficial to wealthy donors and reduce their tax incentives for philanthropy simultaneously, despite that the effective estate tax rate is at a modest level of 17%.[7] A change in government spending could also affect the scale and composition of philanthropy. If public spending is cut in housing, education, research or other areas, a stronger demand for philanthropy would exist to fill the gap.

Foundation endowments have always been intriguing. Trailblazers in philanthropy such as Andrew Carnegie and John D. Rockefeller created institutions that were intended to exist in perpetuity – facilitated by continually growing their original investments. The rise of endowments nurtured growth in asset size. But with a requirement to spend down 5% of assets per year, some have wondered by foundations have been sitting on substantial sums and not using these resources to serve their broader purpose. In recent years, many foundations have explored impact investing and mission-related investments, which harness non-grant assets to invest in issues of concern, seeking a social and financial return.

The Global Impact Investing Network (GIIN)[8] defines impact investments as "investments made into companies, organizations and funds with the intention to generate social and environmental impact alongside a financial return." Impact investment is characterized by the investor's expectation on returns, various return and asset classes, and the impact measurement, which will assess and report the social and environmental performance of the investment. From the perspective of philanthropic organizations, a close concept to impact investment is mission-related investment, which is defined by Confluence Philanthropy[9] as "the practice of harmonizing a charitable organization's mission for social or environmental impact with the management and investment of assets while sustaining long-term financial return".

Key Issues Facing Different Types of Foundations

There is a saying in philanthropy, "When you've seen one foundation, you've seen one foundation." With the highly independent way in which foundations are formed and managed, it is not a surprise that experiences can vary greatly from one foundation to the next. While it is difficult to generalize, there is some value in examining the philanthropic field in segments. While there might not be great commonality between a large private foundation and a small community foundation, there is more in common among community foundations and among large private foundations. This is why cases in this book were identified in categories. This range of foundations has similar and different concerns.

Figure 1.3 shows that since 2002, independent foundations account for about 90% of all the foundations in the U.S. The number of operating and corporate foundations fluctuates at the level of 2,500 and 4,500 respectively; while the number of community foundations sits at less than 1,000 despite its gradual increase in the last decade.

Community foundations represent localities. This is why they were created. But these localities are geographical spaces in which change takes place. Demographics change, industries change. But community foundations remain. They must adapt to their localities to remain relevant. They have to be on top of the issues facing their local communities. They also depend on contributions from donors in their regions. They want to be true to donor intentions, therefore, many community foundations have emphasized DAFs. But they are faced with broader questions about populations beyond donors – the intended beneficiaries of the foundation and other local stakeholders. Some community foundations have become more like anchor institutions or agents of change that use, not only their grantmaking, but their leadership – their voice as a community-based institution – to influence how to improve lives in their regions.

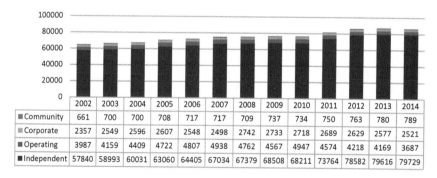

	2002	2003	2004	2005	2006	2007	2008	2009	2010	2011	2012	2013	2014
■ Community	661	700	700	708	717	717	709	737	734	750	763	780	789
▓ Corporate	2357	2549	2596	2607	2548	2498	2742	2733	2718	2689	2629	2577	2521
■ Operating	3987	4159	4409	4722	4807	4938	4762	4567	4947	4574	4218	4169	3687
■ Independent	57840	58993	60031	63060	64405	67034	67379	68508	68211	73764	78582	79616	79729

FIGURE 1.3 Number of Foundation in the U.S. by Type
Source: Foundation Center 2018

In some ways, other types of foundations that are rooted in localities and locally focused in their missions face similar considerations. They are assets in their localities, thereby challenged to consider how they can be greater local actors. Moreover, foundations across the board, are increasingly asked to think beyond their grantmaking – to consider the potential impact of their voices on social issues, leverage their assets beyond grants toward impact investing, and act as collaborators with other foundations, government, and various other partners.

While larger private foundations control substantial assets in philanthropy, small private foundations are greater in number. They may have one staff member or a handful of staff. Their Board of Directors may be comprised of only or mostly family members. They tend to be driven by very personal interests. Yet they exist in an era when foundations are being asked to think differently – to be more transparent and accountable. This affects all foundations, of course. But the dynamics are interesting regarding family foundations, as they are often so closely held. Transparency is typically not the intent. And being challenged on the demographic composition of Boards questions general assumptions about the relative independence of these entities. This category of foundation has the least diversity among Board members, for example.[10]

Large, private foundations are the most known to the general public. Some of them (Ford, Rockefeller, Gates) have recognizable brands. These brands are often well-protected with great attention to communications and reputation. These foundations have powerful voices that can set trends. These institutions have larger staffs. They have more departments and internal systems. Some of them make grants globally. These are complex organizations. The performance of their endowments can shape quite a bit of what they can and cannot do in a given year.

Corporate foundations, while incorporated separately from their corporations, must continually consider alignment between foundation and corporate goals. There are typically structural issues at work in this regard around decision-making. Connecting to consumer bases is an additional matter facing these types of foundations.

The rise of health conversion foundations has created a new category in institutional philanthropy to consider. These foundations emerged from the remaining assets of dissolved health systems. They tend to be created with a mandate to meet health needs of a specific geographic community and include representative Boards of Trustees.

With the wealth that has been created in recent decades due to the growth of new industries, donors are demonstrating various interests in how they would like to contribute. Some eschew the notion of perpetuity, preferring to spend down assets in their lifetimes. Consequently, some foundations that are making substantial gifts are "spend down" foundations, which are not growing endowments to survive for generations. Additionally, it is important to remember that anyone can be philanthropic even if popular conceptions of philanthropy emphasize the wealthy. Lower income communities have been helping each other philanthropically for generations.

Many people of all economic levels make contributions to nonprofit organizations in some capacity. The rise of giving circles, for example, demonstrates ways in which a few people, pooling their resources, can create a grantmaking fund. Private giving can be conducted at every level. As giving for disaster relief can be facilitated by smart phones and crowdsourcing can galvanize contributors to a particular cause or initiative, philanthropy has become further enmeshed into our lives.

Strategic Philanthropy

Strategic philanthropy can be defined as philanthropy used by companies or organizations to benefit their own business interests. Strategic philanthropy often involves specifically targeted philanthropic activities with special issues or causes to be more effective in achieving its commercial or organizational goals. As Brest[11] indicated, "the term strategic philanthropy is treated as synonymous with outcome-oriented, result-oriented, and effective philanthropy".

Strategic philanthropy has attracted attention from scholars and philanthropic practitioners in the last few decades. This could be explained by its prevalence and huge influence on today's philanthropists. As a proponent of strategic philanthropy, Brest[12] suggested that strategic philanthropy could be more efficient and effective utilizing the "expected return mindsets" that could enhance the planning, monitoring and evaluation of philanthropic activities.

The criticisms against strategic philanthropy are also intriguing. Schambra[13] purports that strategic philanthropy is psychologically untenable since the nature of philanthropy is not strategic. As has been summarized by Brest,[14] strategic philanthropy could also be destructive of civil society and difficult to execute. In addition, strategic philanthropy is not the panacea for all different societal issues and cases.

There are also scholars who provide suggestions to improve the effectiveness of strategic philanthropy. Kania et al.[15] argue that strategic philanthropy should shift from a predictive model to an emergent model to address and fit the social complexity, while philanthropic solutions should be kept as simple as possible when solving complex problems.

Inclusion and Strategy

DEI (Diversity, Equity, and Inclusion) in philanthropy mainly includes the following meanings: 1) diversity refers to different groups of people who should be present such as racial and ethnic minority groups, LGBT populations, people with disabilities, etc.; 2) equity means people should be treated fairly within certain philanthropic procedures and for certain resource distribution outcomes; 3) inclusion means certain disadvantaged groups of people should not be excluded or discriminated against.

DEI should be addressed properly due to its critical importance to the success of philanthropy because DEI could make philanthropy more democratic and more effective. However, there are still significant challenges within or out of philanthropy to achieve DEI goals. Chandler[16] mentioned that one of the challenges is that diversity does not necessarily bring inclusiveness, since diversity is only concerned with presence. Inclusivity, on the other hand, requires more comprehensive effort to make different voices equally heard and valued sufficiently.

Furthermore, the leadership of foundations and boards tends to have a slower pace for DEI and therefore restrains the process of organizations or even the whole sector. Specifically, Taylor[17] proposed in the report "The State of Diversity in Environmental Organizations" that the sector needed to take action immediately to diversify its board and staff.

With respect to DEI for global philanthropy, Kuljian's[18] study of philanthropy in South Africa found that most philanthropic funds failed to promote social changes that are necessary for a more equitable society. In other words, the potential function of philanthropy is not realized sufficiently. The study suggested philanthropy should be used to address the structural issue of inequality, such as supporting nongovernment organizations in enhancing the roles of unfavored groups of people in allocating resources; and devoting philanthropic resources to help improve the capacity of local organizations in social justice and transformation.

Philanthropy continues to evolve, and grapple with its role. And it includes a wide range of highly participatory and inclusive approaches along with decidedly individualistic and egotistical manifestations. Through the efforts of my company, Marga Incorporated, a consulting firm providing strategic advice and research to philanthropic initiatives and community partnerships, I have observed numerous methods. Marga has advised multiple foundations, large and small, over the last couple of decades. There is no singular answer to whether philanthropy is a genuine avenue to civic participation and necessary social change. However, the field includes a great deal of intellectual capital, passion, and a desire for improvement. While innovative thinking may be stifled by rigid institutional practices in some cases, some very compelling philanthropic strategies are emerging.

One matter that is important to note is that these innovations demonstrate that philanthropic institutions bring more than money. The Cleveland Foundation in Cleveland, Ohio in the United States created the Greater University Circle Initiative. This effort combines the resources and expertise of multiple local anchor institutions, which are enduring organizations playing a central role in their communities and economies. The Cleveland Foundation's President, Ronn Richard, approached the presidents of some of the local anchor institutions, such as Case Western Reserve University, The Cleveland Clinic, and University Hospitals. He asked them to join together to address multiple issues in their locality jointly, along with local government. This led to an ongoing partnership that is improving housing, transportation, employment, and other issues in the geographical area they share in common. This example demonstrates the ability of a philanthropic institution, in this case, a community foundation, to facilitate the development of an entirely new initiative and approach to community improvement. Through this ability to convene, the foundation not only harnessed its own capital; it leveraged capital from other institutions on behalf of civil society. This approach to inclusion was informed by a recognition of the limitations of a singular foundation's resources, and a desire to craft a joint strategy with other local institutions with a vested interest in the conditions of the city they all share.

Marga Incorporated spent some years working with another community foundation in New Haven, Connecticut – the Community Foundation for Greater New Haven. Among its many funds established by donors was the Urban Prosperity Fund, which focused on the needs of the African American community in the region. Over time, the fund evolved into the idea for an entire foundation, based on the community foundation model, which addresses the needs of African Americans in the entire state of Connecticut, called The Prosperity Foundation (TPF). This effort offers opportunities for donors interested in strengthening the African American community in areas such as health, education, and economic development to donate to TPF or establish a fund at TPF based on their interests. This effort demonstrates a participatory population-based model of philanthropy designed to involve the African American community (and others) in improving its own standing through a philanthropic vehicle.

The Community Foundation for Greater New Haven secured a grant from the W.K. Kellogg Foundation, a large private foundation, to support TPF's development. Kellogg is investing in multiple philanthropic innovations designed to improve communities of color across the United States through its Catalyzing Community Giving initiative. This effort is demonstrating how a well-endowed longstanding private foundation can influence the development of local philanthropy by and for communities often underrepresented in receiving substantial philanthropic dollars. This historical underrepresentation represents one of the ways in which philanthropy has not been inclusive. The Kellogg Foundation, in this instance has created a space to strengthen efforts that intend to fill this void, and design strategies that are driven by the perspectives of constituents that have not been adequately included in philanthropy.

Another well-endowed private foundation, the Ford Foundation recently reflected on its history, impact, and value to inform the development of a new point of emphasis. The Ford Foundation's president invited input on the foundation's work, and received two thousand emails. Incorporating suggestions from a wide network into how the foundation gives and reflecting on growing disparities around the globe, the foundation decided to focus its energies on reducing inequality. Their approach to giving will emphasize deeper partnerships with grantees in six priority areas, providing levels and types of support that will better enable financial stability. This example demonstrates the ability of a major foundation to open up lines of communication to include its constituency to inform decision making.

Since 2006, Marga Inc. has been coordinating the Race and Equity in Philanthropy Group (REPG), which brings together foundations of varying types to discuss how their institutions craft inclusive policies and practices. As the philanthropic industry has grown, so has the role of foundations as employers, purchasers, and grantmakers. Foundations have been increasingly scrutinized for their lack of diversity. As demographics in civil society shift, so does philanthropy's responsibility to reflect the composition of the communities in which it is working. Furthermore, it is becoming increasingly clear that foundation policies and practices are a reflection of who sits in positions of leadership. Looking to the future, we must wonder about the significance of the composition of foundation leadership in influencing philanthropy's role in civil society. And these dynamics are very much shaped by the nature and scope of foundations. For example, small family foundations tend to be governed by family members, while larger private foundations without living donors have greater room to diversify. But the persistence of racial inequities and the increasingly public dialogue about these dynamics raises questions about the relevance of philanthropic institutions to this discussion. And if foundations are going to be more effective at addressing matters of race and inclusion, it seems the voices of communities of color should be essential in constructing and maintaining the strategies, systems, and programs that would reduce racial disparities and expand racial justice. Indeed, one of the more robust conversations about innovating philanthropy to increase impact is about the capacity of foundations to genuinely reflect and impact diverse communities.

I will say more about REPG later in the book. The methodology of this group leverages peer learning as a way to influence institutional change in foundations. Many foundations are influenced by practices in other philanthropic institutions. Lessons that can be drawn from the practices and experiences of a single foundation can be instructive to practices in other foundations. This is the spirit that informed the idea for this book — to highlight how a range of different foundations are seeking to be more equitable and inclusive in practice. Ultimately, if we are to envision institutional change that leads to more equitable and inclusive foundations, we must understand the techniques, methods, approaches, and tactics that allow these concepts to materialize.

The foundations profiled in this book are, as many of them indicate, on a "journey" to challenge traditions, reframe their thinking, and rearrange their work to be inclusively strategic. These six foundations are, admittedly, far from finished products. But they have all demonstrated some degree of courage in reflecting upon the relevance of their work, and engaging constituents in new ways. If we are to imagine change in philanthropy that embraces new values and transcends traditional limitations, we must be able to understand tangible manifestations of the principles to which many aspire. In order for philanthropy to transcend, philanthropists and foundations must begin to change. The six foundations profiled in the pages to follow exhibit some specific ways in which foundations can innovate and begin to transform. Their experiences provide us with insights that can be useful in our understanding of the role of philanthropy in society now and into the future.

Notes

1 Philanthropy's response to the bankruptcy settlement of Detroit is very timely and overwhelmingly positive. In 2014, Detroit local foundations and philanthropists pledged over $330 million, an unprecedented scale of philanthropic aid to cities, to save the Detroit Institute of Arts collection from being sold off to pay the unfunded pension liabilities. In addition to the pension pool, some foundations such as Kresge have also attempted to help the ravaged neighborhoods in Detroit to regain their economic and community development via a series of groundbreaking initiatives. For example, the Detroit Future City Plan, which was jointly presented by Kresge and other foundations, was developed meticulously after consulting with local residents and community leaders.
2 (Casey 2016)
3 Ibid.
4 (Johnson 2010)
5 (Johnson 2017: 14)
6 (National Philanthropic Trust 2017)
7 (Center on Budget and Policy Priorities 2017)
8 (Global Impact Investing Network 2018)
9 (Confluence Philanthropy 2018)
10 According to the Urban Institutes' Family Philanthropy's 2015 Trend Study by Boris et al. (2015), for over 70% of all the family foundations in the U.S., family members make up at least 75% of the foundation board; and first and second generation family members are the major family groups on the board of family foundations.
11 (Brest 2015)
12 Ibid.
13 (Schambra 2008)
14 (Brest 2015)
15 (Kania et al. 2014)
16 (Chandler et al. 2014)
17 (Taylor 2014)
18 (Kuljian 2005)

References

Boris, T.E., Carol J. De Vita, and Marcus Gaddy. *National Center for Family Philanthropy's 2015 Trends Study*. 2015. http://www.ncfp.org/permalink/063c7342-92bc-11e5-8f77-00224d7a 7b28.pdf (accessed September 20, 2018).

Brest, Paul. "Strategic philanthropy and its discontents." *Stanford Social Innovation Review*, April 27, 2015. https://ssir.org/up_for_debate/article/strategic_philanthropy_and_its_ discontents# (accessed September 20, 2018).

Casey, John. "Comparing nonprofit sectors around the world: What do we know and how do we know it?" *The Journal of Nonprofit Education and Leadership* 6, no. 3. 2016.

Center on Budget and Policy Priorities. *Policy Basics: the Federal Estate Tax*. 2017. https://www. cbpp.org/sites/default/files/atoms/files/policybasics-estatetax.pdf/ (accessed September 14, 2018).

Chandler, A., L. Quay, and T.A. Martinez. *Philanthropic Paths: An Exploratory Study of Career Pathways for Professionals of Color in Philanthropy*. Chicago: D5 Coalition. 2014.

Confluence Philanthropy. *What Is Mission-Related Investing/ Impact Investing?*2018. http:// www.confluencephilanthropy.org/What-Is-Mission/Impact-Investing (accessed September 15, 2018).

Foundation Center. *Foundation Stats*. 2018. http://data.foundationcenter.org/#/founda tions/ (accessed September 10, 2018).

Global Impact Investing Network, GIIN. *What is Impact Investing?*2018. https://thegiin. org/impact-investing/need-to-know/#what-is-impact-investing (accessed October 1, 2018).

Johnson, Paula D. *Global Institutional Philanthropy: A Preliminary Status Report*. World Wide Initiatives for Grantmaker Support and the Philanthropic Initiative, Inc.2010.

Johnson, Paula D. *The Global Philanthropy Report: Perspectives on the Global Foundation Sector*. Harvard Kennedy School, the Hauser Institute for Civil Society at the Center for Public Leadership, 2017.

Kania, John, Mark Kramer, and Patty Russell. "Strategic philanthropy for a complex world." *Stanford Social Innovation Review* 12, no. 3(2014): 26–33.

Kuljian, Christa L. "Philanthropy and equity: The case of South Africa". Global Equity Initiative: Harvard University. 2005.

National Center for Charitable Statistics. *The Non-profit Sector in Brief*. 2016. https://nccs. urban.org/ (accessed September 10, 2018).

National Philanthropic Trust. *2017 Donor-Advised Fund Report*. 2017. https://www.np trust.org/daf-report/ (accessed September 11, 2018).

Schambra, William. "The problem of strategic philanthropy". In *Philanthropy Roundtable Annual Meeting*. 2008. https://www.hudson.org/content/researchattachments/attachm ent/677/2008_11_07_schambra_on_strategic_philanthropy.pdf (accessed September 15, 2018).

Taylor, Dorceta E. *The State of Diversity in Environmental Organizations*. Ann Arbor, MI: University of Michigan. 2014.

2

PRIVATE FOUNDATIONS

Meyer Memorial Trust

Background on the Foundation

As a charitable trust under the laws of Oregon, Meyer Memorial Trust was created in 1982 by Fred G. Meyer, who founded a chain of retail stores throughout the Pacific Northwest. The Trust was originally named, Fred Meyer Charitable Trust, and subsequently changed to Meyer Memorial Trust in 1990 in order to clearly distinguish the Trust from the commercial enterprise Fred Meyer, Inc. As a locally engaged trust, the grants awarded by Meyer have covered all of Oregon's 36 counties, and 80% of cities, communities and unincorporated places in the state.

Due to Fred Meyer's intentional open-ended language in his will, the Meyer Memorial Trust has a rare amount of flexibility to adjust its giving strategy to the ever-changing needs of Oregon's communities. Mr. Meyer was aware that he could not foresee the most necessary areas that would need support. "Realizing as I do the uncertainties of the future, I want my trustees to be able to exercise broad discretion in shaping and carrying out charitable programs which can be tailored to fit changing conditions and problems," Meyer stated in his will. This is a significant and visionary statement that is not typical of donors creating foundations. From the outset, the Meyer Memorial Trust was established as a relatively independent private foundation.

According to the Trust's Consolidated Financial Statements 2018,[1] for the year ended March 31, 2018, Meyer's assets reached over US$790 million with annual grant giving at a total of $36.56 million. The total contribution from the Estate Fred G. Meyer has aggregated $126,199,492 since its formation. To September 2019, Meyer has granted over $786 million in total through more than 9,440 individual or series of grants and program related investments in the last 37 years.[2] The Trust has around 40 staff members.[3]

The Trust's open-ended guidelines have helped enable Meyer to weave an authentic commitment to equity into the fabric of the foundation. The Trust's mission is "to work with and invest in organizations, communities, ideas and efforts that contribute to a flourishing and equitable Oregon."[4] Equity, which Meyer defines as "fair access to opportunities,"[5] is also stressed as one of the six primary aspects of Meyer's vision and values, along with responsiveness and flexibility, collaboration, humbleness, accountability and transparency, and advocacy.[6]

The Trust underwent an executive transition during the period in which it was identified as a subject for this book. When this research began, Doug Stamm was the CEO. Stamm, a white male, joined the Trust in 2002. He has a lengthy working history in the state of Oregon. He was aware that he was stepping down from this position when we interviewed him for this book. Of his departure, he said, "One of the reasons why I feel like it's the right time for me to leave is that I've taken it to where I can."[7] He was making reference to the foundation's ongoing effort to increase its commitment to diversity, equity, and inclusion. In 2013, Stamm as an individual and the Trust as a whole embarked on "a shared equity journey" that resulted from a review of their mission and values.[8] It was the voices of staff, who expressed their lived experiences, which gave Stamm a sense of urgency regarding equity. For Stamm, this was "an urgency to make a personal and foundational commitment to dismantle bias and inequity in his home state."[9]

The Trust's current CEO is Michelle J. DePass. DePass, an African-American woman who joined the foundation officially in April of 2018. She was previously at the Ford Foundation as a Program Officer creating funding initiatives at the intersection of environmental justice and community and economic development. Just prior to joining Meyer, she was a Dean at the New School's Milano School of International Affairs, Management and Urban Policy. She was also an assistant administrator at the U.S. Environmental Protection Agency under the Obama administration. Upon the announcement of DePass's hiring, the Trust's Board Chair at the time, Charles Wilhoite wrote, "Michelle has sought out and excelled in roles where she can make a difference and shift the power dynamic to improve life for people of color, women, indigenous peoples, and low-income communities."[10] In a statement, DePass said, upon her hiring, "Meyer Memorial Trust believes that everyone in Oregon deserves to live in a safe place, that the educational experience that we provide for our children will provide a world of opportunity, that the environment surrounding us should be a source of strength and richness, and that our communities sustain us with a sense of belonging and possibility, regardless of race or class." She continued, "For this to happen and make Oregon an equitable place, we must dismantle systemic oppression and have the discipline to ask ourselves over and over again: does this decision remove barriers or reinforce them? I am joining Meyer's dedicated board, committed staff and fellows and innovative grantees to remove those barriers. That is how we expand opportunity."[11]

The hiring of someone of DePass's background and perspective is a continuation of the equity journey that was launched in 2013. During that time, the entire staff of the foundation became more diverse as well. DePass emphasizes the removal of barriers as a central feature of how the Trust can contribute to its communities. It is clear that Meyer is addressing equity both externally in how it engages local communities and internally regarding its composition, policies, practices, and internal culture. Stamm helped begin a process, and DePass arrived to guide the foundation through a next phase.

Considerations for Private Foundations

On the surface, one might assume the Trust is a family foundation. It was created in 1982 by an individual after whom the organization is named. Although the founder is not living, one might assume his heirs would be the majority of Board members. Private foundations are typically entities that may have been started by an individual or family, but are largely governed by non-family members. Many of the more well-known foundations, such as the Ford and Rockefeller Foundations, while once extensions of their founders, are now governed and staffed by non-family members. The content of many family foundations' programming is often closely aligned with the will of the founder or founding family. Many private foundations[12] feel relatively free to shape their priorities well beyond an original charter. Private foundations often have the flexibility to adapt to changing times and alter the substance of their efforts accordingly. When the staff of a foundation wants to encourage risk and pursue perspectives and programs that might be considered controversial, a flexible institutional mandate it useful. The executive leadership of Meyer is not beholden to a highly specialized will and testament. It is in fact, encouraged by the original donor to evolve with the times.

When asked about the nature of the Trust as a private foundation despite being named after a founding individual, former CEO, Doug Stamm replied, "One of the things that concerned me when I came in was where is the accountability and where is the urgency. Mr. Meyer is no longer alive and we need to be accountable for his intention, and we need to be accountable for the stakeholders across the state."[13] This is one of the significant challenges facing many foundations – the combination of honoring the wishes of a founder as well as remaining relevant to the current needs of the times and the specific constituencies of interest to the foundation. Stamm continued, "We are not a family foundation, but when Mr. Meyer died, he had no direct heirs. The original Board of Trustees were primarily business associates of Fred Meyer. So, we are not a family foundation; but given the size of the board which was always five but currently it is six, it resembles a family foundation."[14] This is a circumstance in which the founder had no heirs. It appears that the Trust never really operated as a family foundation. Indeed, the Board members were colleagues of the founder, but not family members. Stamm pointed out the size of the Board, giving the Trust the feel of a family foundation. Currently, Meyer has only five Trustees.[15]

As Stamm wondered about accountability and urgency, it appears, the Trust had the latitude to reflect and engage its constituents in order to inform the foundation's strategic direction rather than concern itself only with a mandate from a deceased founder. This is one of the benefits of a private foundation, which is not a family foundation. This may be particularly advantageous when a foundation wants to pursue an unconventional path and potentially depart significantly from longstanding programmatic priorities or methods of operating. When a foundation wants to embark on a journey to become more diverse, equitable, and inclusive, for example, it is likely going to have to challenge itself. It is going to have to reflect and change. Moreover, this change, to varying degrees, takes time. The Meyer Memorial Trust recognizes this reality, and is continuing on its equity journey.

Strategy – The Essence of the Foundation's Strategy

The current mission of the Trust, and the foundation's emphasis on diversity, equity, and inclusion represented a change in direction, which was further refined in 2016. In 2017, the Trust was recognized for this change by the National Committee on Responsive Philanthropy (NCRP). NCRP distributes *Impact Awards* in various categories, one of which is "Changing Course" that is awarded to foundations that have been exemplary at incorporating feedback to inform their efforts. Doug Stamm indicated in response to receiving this award, "Meyer's journey would not have been possible without the patience, advice, and partnership of many Oregon-based nonprofits. We take input from our stakeholders seriously; those working directly on behalf of Oregonians most affected by inequity and injustice serve as models and teachers for our philanthropy."[16]

In the wake of President Trump's election, protests in Charlottesville, and other current events that highlighted the need for attention to diversity, equity, and inclusion, the Trust reinforced its internal and external equity efforts, which were initiated in 2013. A commitment to equity is a fundamental aspect of the Trust's strategic direction. This point of emphasis stresses the dismantling of barriers to greater equity for communities across the state of Oregon. As indicated on their website, "We prioritize work that increases equity for and inclusion of Oregonians who experience disparities because of race, ethnicity, national origin, citizenship status, religion, gender, gender identity, sexual orientation, class, disability status, geographic location or age."[17] The trust is explicit about the range of demographics that it is considering when it pursues greater equity. It is naming some of the ways in which communities are presented with barriers to opportunities. The trust also indicates its desire for nonprofit organizations in Oregon to embark on an equity journey along with them. Meyer's equity journey includes direct self-examination about the degree to which it upholds principles of

diversity, equity, and inclusion in their own foundation, and encouraging organizations in Oregon communities to do the same. Indeed, if greater equity in the
region is the goal, the nonprofit organizations serving local communities would
have to share this thinking about an equity journey.

As equity is a theme cutting across all of the foundation's efforts externally and
internally, their approach includes a few dimensions. Their mission to bring about
greater equity in Oregon is implemented through grant making in four program
areas: Building Community, Equitable Education, Healthy Environment, and
Housing Opportunities. In pursuing these substantive areas of interest, the foundation is highlighting the need to address the systems and policies that can create
and reinforce the very barriers to equity it seeks to dissolve. The trust recognizes
that this is a long process. Therefore, short-term grantmaking is not their primary
focus. This is an important feature in foundations considering a commitment to
equity and inclusion in their programming. This is not work with easy solutions.
They are complex, challenging issues that take time to address.

While Meyer focuses on particular program areas, it is also committed to
remaining open to adaptation where necessary. The foundation asserts, "We
challenge ourselves and our partners to take risks and to adapt to changing community conditions and needs as they evolve."[18] Their willingness to publicize
their appetite for risk is intriguing for any foundation. While many foundations
are probably more positioned to take risks than organizations in other fields, risk
aversion is a more common approach. This interest also demonstrates Meyer's
willingness to allow the conditions in communities drive their thinking and
action. This is where engagement with the communities it hopes to help improve
is essential. It is difficult to truly understand conditions in communities and adapt
accordingly without effective lines of communication with the organizations serving those particular populations. Meyer's website states, "We believe that collaboration with nonprofit organizations, those they serve and other key partners
and stakeholders is essential to our effectiveness. We support strategies that elevate
community-based knowledge and the voices of communities experiencing disparities to shape decisions that affect them."[19] Respect for the perspectives of
those with lived experiences with disparities is something Meyer has come to
appreciate and prioritize. In this approach, their role as a grant-making entity is
not merely distributing funds to nonprofit organizations in a few select program
areas. It is a matter of co-creating the work – partnering with community-based
organizations as well as the constituents they serve in order to arrive at proposed
solutions.

Additionally, the Trust sees themselves as "conveners", who can bring together
various stakeholders to discuss the issues facing communities and appropriate
strategies to address them. Meyer prioritizes learning, and also supports research
and evaluation. Grantees of the foundation have the opportunity to participate in
"shared learning" to facilitate greater understanding of the work.[20] Meyer also
supports technical assistance for grantees. Finally, Meyer also engages in "strategic

communications, advocacy, mission investing, and leverage".[21] These components illustrate how the Trust's approach far transcends grant-making. Meyer is maximizing uses of their assets to leverage funds and resources from elsewhere and making greater use of their financial assets through mission investing. The breadth of their approach is multifaceted.

When asked about how the foundation arrived at this equity-focused approach to their work, Stamm responded, "We kept coming back to the long-existing and growing disparities between people of color and other historically marginalized groups and that helped us to answer the question that has been raised when we did our new vision and values which was, to contribute to a more flourishing and equitable Oregon. Trying to define and recognizing where we really were not being effective was closing these consistent disparities."[22] Their process to develop their strategy told them that barriers still exist. These barriers especially persisted for particular demographic groups. Meyer recognized it needed to change. It seems they grappled with where their work had not been successful, and concluded that a commitment to equity and inclusion would have to be central to their mission and purpose. It would have to be demonstrated in their programs as well as their policies and practices.

How Inclusion Informs Strategy Programmatically

As previously noted, in 2016, the Trust divided its programmatic giving into four issue-focused and equity-based portfolios: Building Community, Equitable Education, Healthy Environment, and Housing Opportunities. In particular, these portfolios are intended to address equity and justice issues in community development, reduce the achievement gap in education, improve the health of the ecosystem and environment protection efforts, overcome substandard housing conditions, and guarantee fair housing and equal access.

Building Community "is working toward a just, complex, multicultural society where everyone can thrive."[23] This portfolio supports organizations that maintain an explicit commitment to diversity, equity, and inclusion; remain accountable to their communities; and are able to connect to systems' change efforts.

Equitable Education funds "organizations, institutions, and networks that improve outcomes for student populations experiencing disparities in educational opportunity and achievement."[24] In particular, this portfolio is addressing systems and policy-level change in education as well as student achievement and college and career readiness. They are intentionally supporting efforts in both urban and rural areas in this effort and stressing an equity lens to analyze disparities and work to dismantle them.

Healthy Environment seeks to "protect and improve the health and resiliency of Oregon's natural environment…"[25] It also focuses on the systems and structures that prevent particular populations from gaining access to a healthy environment. This portfolio explicitly seeks to support community-led efforts that emphasize equitably distributed access to environmental benefits and impacts, support a movement for a healthy environment, and ensure the resilience of natural systems.

Housing Opportunities envisions "that every Oregonian has a safe, decent, affordable place to call home."[26] This portfolio seeks to address racist and discriminatory housing policies that prevent access to quality housing for particular populations. It funds efforts that increase the availability of affordable housing units, the stability of housing for particular populations, and stronger, more equitable housing systems and strategies.

All four of these program areas are framed within a commitment to equity. Furthermore, guidelines for grant seekers in each of these areas include explicit statements regarding equity. In these four areas combined are issues that are fundamental necessities for all populations, but are not distributed equitably.

How Inclusion Informs Strategy Institutionally

Meyer's commitment to equity and inclusion is most pronounced in the foundation's internal systems, operations, policies, procedures, and composition. The equity journey that Meyer embarked upon was intended to, not only, shape programming and external engagement with constituents. It was very important to the foundation that it could reflect their values as an institution. One significant institutional decision was to hire their first Director of Human Resources to support equity efforts for new and existing staff. Today, half of the staff and trustees identify as people of color and a number represent other marginalized communities. The foundation placed a high priority on ensuring the foundation would resemble their equitable and inclusive vision.

Not only has the staff become more diverse; the composition of the Board has changed dramatically. As of 2019, Meyer had more trustees of color than white trustees and the board chair is a black woman. In addition, the entire executive team identifies as female, and a majority are women of color. Stamm said of their development into a more diverse, equitable, and inclusive organization, "When I came here the Board was all white and primarily male, the group of trustees has placed equity and inclusion top of the organization as priority... From a grant-making stand point, we very much look like a social justice organization."[27] Their experiences and transformation illustrate the many facets of an organization that must be considered in order to live its values. This is well beyond the rhetorical. And, for foundations, this transcends grant making. Programmatic and institutional transformation go hand-in-hand. They are mutually reinforcing. Bringing in community representation with lived experiences in the issue areas the foundation is trying to address, helps the foundation more effectively fulfill its mission. Who is at the table makes a difference in how a foundation, or any organization, establishes its priorities and implements its work. According to

Stamm, their frame of thinking on inclusion inside of the organization is informed by, "The Acronym PAAIO (who are the People at the table making decisions; what are the Assumptions before making decisions; Authority, where the final decision maker lies; question the Intentions; and One voice)."[28] This is an interesting way of considering not only the composition of a group but the full participation of people in the group. It captures the essence of the distinction between diversity alone without inclusion and equity. The PAAIO approach encompasses the continuum from representation to actual participation in decision making and clarity of purpose. This framework can help diagnose where actual power resides and understand how to change in order to become more diverse, equitable, and inclusive.

The kind of comprehensive institutional change taking place at Meyer is not episodic. There are no single events that are instant solutions. The change is continuous and, in fact, unceasing. Because this is an exercise in continuous reflection, innovations, and renewal. With this reality in mind, the Trust created a Diversity, Equity, and Inclusion Working Group (DEIWG) which is now called the Equity Team. This team was instrumental in transitioning the organization during its strategic redesign. We interviewed two members of the Equity Team – Cristina Watson and Karissa Lowe. Cristina Watson was a Program Officer for Willamette River Initiative, a ten-year project that shifted to become an independent, community-driven collaborative in 2019 called the Willamette River Network. Lowe is Meyer's Knowledge and Data Manager. She joined Meyer in 2007. A member of the Cowlitz Indian Tribe, Lowe has served as an at-Large Representative on the Tribal Council for 15 years.

The original Working Group, and subsequently, the Equity Team have played the role of an internal catalyst or guide with focused attention on ensuring the Trust is demonstrating a commitment to its values throughout the organization. Kimberly A.C. Wilson, the foundation's Director of Communications, also participated in this interview. She has been at Meyer since 2014. She is a member of the Meyer's Executive Team. Her work involves managing the foundation's voice in the philanthropic sector. She reflected on the role of the Working Group in the equity journey. She said, "From my perspective, we wouldn't be where we are as an organization without what the equity team and DEIWG did to guide this organization to be where we are and normalize how equity fits into the work. I agree that we are on this journey, but I think in a very short amount of time, they are responsible for allowing us to leapfrog in terms of how we think and process the value of this work."[29] The working group model allowed for a group of representatives in the foundation to reflect upon and determine how the Trust could actualize various aspects along their equity journey. Wilson makes an important point about the ability of a dedicated formation within the organization to accelerate institutional change. Indeed, the process of institutional transformation is lengthy and continuous, but their working group model helped them advance from concepts to new practices. Her reference to "normalize" is also intriguing, as it speaks to the paradigmatic shift required – a shift from one way of operating, which is almost cultural and embedded to another. This is no small task.

Watson referenced the cultural shift that has been underway, stating, "There's a culture here doing this work that is hugely different than when I started which is a huge benefit. Whether or not it's because of the E-Team – I don't know – but the E-Team has certainly contributed to that."[30] Watson doesn't wholly attribute the cultural change to the internal group, now the Equity Team, but she can see an evolution from where they were upon her arrival at the foundation to where they are now. She specifically indicated a "cultural shift", underscoring the depth of the transformation. It is not only that they have different people, the way they operate on the whole has been taking on a different shape.

Previously, the Equity Team was comprised of representatives from different departments in the foundation. It includes thematic subgroups – Communications, Human Resources, Ongoing Learning, Emerging Issues, Speakers Bureau, Documenting our Journey, Equity Journey. The Equity Team is considering developing a subgroup on Vendors. This variation in subgroups enables participation from various constituents inside of Meyer. These subgroups capture many aspects of the Trust's work, acknowledging the comprehensiveness of an equity journey – it would have to touch all dimensions of the foundation in order to authentically transform the institution. In Communications, they are able to address how they discuss their commitment to these values externally. Human Resources provides a space for them to address recruitment into the foundation, opportunities for advancement, and the working and decision-making culture in the institution. Emerging Issues allows for discussion about new issues that might surface. In their other subgroups, they are taking into account how they learn from their progress and challenges as well as how they are able to continually capture points of progress in their efforts.

It seems they made an important decision to allow the original working group to help establish equity as a priority and begin to influence cultural change, and then further embed this function through the ongoing efforts of the Equity Team. The presence of this Team not only informs policies and practices, it is an avenue to incorporate staff across the foundation at all levels in the process. Karissa Lowe said of participation from across the foundation, that "Anyone, at any level can be a part of a team and participate in a way that's meaningful to them is important...We want the E-team to support staff members in feeling like they can own a piece of the equity work."[31]

The Equity Team allows for discussion on how equity is manifested in the Trust internally and externally, and appears flexible enough in its subgroup model to identify other aspects of equity to address over time. Since the beginning of their equity journey in 2013, the foundation looks and acts differently – closer to a vision for equity that it began to craft years ago.

Progress – What Has Been the Impact of these Approaches? How is Progress Measured?

Clearly, the foundation has progressed along its equity journey in how it appears and how it behaves culturally. Stamm reflected on some of the ways the foundation members have progressed since the inception of their equity journey, "In terms of the progress made in the last five years: 1) demographics, the richness and diversity of the organization; 2) direct impact and shift of the founding and founding approaches; 3) we are pushing the field. We have raised the awareness (of equity) both in the foundation but also the nonprofit field."[32] For Stamm, the impact has been both internal and external. He recognizes many of the aforementioned changes in demographics and practice as a foundation. Here he adds the dimension of their influence in the field. There are lessons to be learned from a transformative process such as the one Meyer has been experiencing, which can be instructive to other places. The aforementioned Impact Award from NCRP was one example of how the Meyer story has been highlighted in the broader field.

Since Meyer embarked on its equity journey in 2013, it is a different foundation. It is more demographically diverse, but also systemically more inclusive. Its Equity Team establishes the function to allow diverse voices in the institution to help shape the Trust's direction. Its Board is more diverse as well, which has an influence on its thinking about its priorities as an institution, including how the foundation identified and selected a CEO, who is a woman of color with an explicit commitment to diversity, equity, and inclusion. It rearranged its level of commitment to these principles, and then gradually began to institute new policies and practices, which began to change the culture.

As Meyer recognizes they are on a journey, continuous dialogue and reflection helps it assess its progress. Programmatically, the foundation created committees to assess progress for each portfolio. The CEO sits on each of these committees, which involve Trustees as well. Stamm indicated, "At least two trustees are assigned to [each portfolio] and we meet quarterly in addition to the regular whole board meeting. Much of that time is spent on learning opportunities to evaluation and progress reports."[33] Additionally, applications are required to address diversity, equity, and inclusion in their proposals. Meyer has developed a tool to rate organizations based on this information. Watson said of this system, "It's a supportive tool that is forward looking so it is more encouraging. Could also be used as a self-evaluation tool too."[34] As Meyer's pursuit is to change culture internally, it is also in the position to influence an equity journey externally. Organizations look to foundations for resources. They represent the communities that foundations hope to improve. However, there are no guarantees that grantee organizations are committed to the same values; they very well might not be particularly diverse, equitable, or inclusive. Meyer has developed a system to embed their values into how they interface with grantees and provide an avenue for grantees to consider how to deepen their own commitment to these principles within their work.

While the Trust has been recognized externally for its institutional transformation, Watson spoke to a sense of desire to continually improve. She said, "We want people working at the foundation to have the ability to work at a place that lives up to its external reputation."[35] This sense of desire to continually enhance and build upon the values and practices it has been developing over recent years is an important feature in understanding how the Trust approaches its commitment to diversity, equity, and inclusion. But this is not to suggest that each foundation representative thinks exactly the same about the direction of Meyer's work going forward. Lowe suggested, "A lot of people would ask what are you trying to accomplish? Each person on the team would have a different answer."[36] Therefore, Meyer's stakeholders have shared values and a broad sense of how they would like to continue to design and refine programs, policies, and practices. However, there is not total uniformity about exactly how to implement. Institutional change, in many ways, is dealing with the unknown.

Learning

With this uncertainty comes learning. The foundation committed to a journey. Recognizing that this path is neither linear not easily traveled is a part of the process. Stamm became increasingly aware of these challenges as the foundation embarked on this path. He said, "To dramatically shift an organization that has been in dominant culture for years is a heavy lift and it comes with struggles. There's no book. There's no how to book to get it right."[37] As he indicated, there is no clear roadmap that one can consult in order to pursue this level of change. In addition to the preexisting cultural and systemic power dynamics Stamm referenced, every foundation and every foundation's constituency has some unique qualities. Lessons arise from trial and error with a recognition of context.

The learning process, like the equity journey, does not end. Recognizing this reality is crucial to a foundation's ability to become truly transformative. When a foundation embraces learning, it is positioned to appreciate the totality of the journey. It is certainly useful to document progress, which also means capturing the full scope of successes as well as challenges. Stamm said, "As an organization we are also documenting our equity work and progress...We have lots of learning opportunities around equity all the time."[38] The reference to "learning opportunities" here illustrates a willingness to allow challenges or even failures to inform the direction going forward.

Some of this thinking is counter to some paradigms in foundation culture. Many foundations, for example, seek quick results and seek to reduce complex problems to highly specified measurable outcomes. Additionally, many foundations organize their programming in this manner to limit risk. An equity journey, like the one embraced by Meyer is neither quick nor risk averse, and it is usually not easily measurable in every dimension. Certainly, a foundation can reach out to a greater number of grantees or add more persons of color to its staff. Some goals are conducive to quantitative measurement. But the breadth of cultural change within a foundation and regarding how a philanthropic institution engages externally is multidimensional and sometimes hard to quantify. Meyer's commitment to learning along a lengthy equity journey is a wise disposition, as there are likely many additional opportunities to learn in the years to come.

Direction and Conclusions

Doug Stamm was on the verge of departing the foundation upon the time he was interviewed for this book. As he envisioned the future of Meyer's equity journey during our discussion, he said, "I think from the organizational stand point you can just expect things need to be evolved. What I can feel confident about is with the makeup of the trustees, the makeup of staff, the leader shifting…that combination will continue to refine, improve and evaluate the work as we get enough time and space."[39] The composition of the foundation's leadership and staff, and the content of the work itself are inextricable in Stamm's view. Stamm's leadership, it appears, was an initial phase in the journey, which emphasized institutionalizing a commitment to diversity, equity, and inclusion. Including a greater number of people of color with lived experiences and a commitment to these values was one important aspect of an earlier phase in this journey. As the journey moves toward a more comprehensive cultural change in the organization, the people involved play an essential role. By establishing an internal formation – the Equity Team – to enable the entire staff to participate in shaping the next steps in the journey, a function was developed to maximize the diversification of the staff. Changing the composition of the Board was also a significant step, because the level of governance and policy making are shaped by new and more diverse perspectives as well.

Lowe and Watson elaborated on some aspects that need greater attention into the next phases of the journey. Lowe pointed to the need for "clear lines of communication and definitions of success".[40] Watson added, "Clearly defined roles and accountability measures…" She continued, "A lot of that has to do with where Meyer is at as an organization. We have almost doubled in size. We are still trying to figure out who we are and how we are trying to do it."[41] As longtime staff members at the foundation and participants in the Equity Team, they have witnessed and helped shape many changes at Meyer. They both indicated the need for greater clarity as a priority for the next phase of the equity journey. This is a next level of institutionalizing their commitment – greater clarity about what they are seeking, roles, and accountability. As they are deeper into their journey, conceptions of what success means to them have evolved. Even with the significant ways in which the foundation has grown and developed over recent years, there is still much more to be done.

Another way in which Watson sees the foundation building on its equity journey is through greater attention externally. She said, "I see in the next few years for the E-Team's projects to start really becoming community facing and being less focused on incorporating it institutionally."[42] This is a compelling perspective, which underscores how Meyer approached its initial phase of their equity journey. Meyer emphasized its own composition and internal systems to position itself to live its values as an organization. Watson sees the opportunity to increasingly stress an approach that more directly interfaces with external constituents.

With the various internal changes already instituted at the Trust, one change it did not make was hiring someone with the sole responsibility of monitoring the foundation's commitment to equity. For Lowe, this is something she would like to see in the future. She said, "I would love to see a full-time equity officer whose job was to go to the executive team meetings and keep the lines of communication open."[43] Watson elaborated on this idea, highlighting the intentional reason they have not yet created such a position. She said, "There was an intentional non-hire at the beginning of the journey. There are pitfalls usually at other organizations when they hire someone right away. Then, the equity work gets put on them. If it's not getting done, then it's their fault."[44]

This is a significant point demonstrating their awareness of the potential danger of placing too much pressure on a single person before the idea of a commitment to equity is further embedded in the systems, practices, and culture of the organization. While such a position might still be necessary, they made the decision to allow the foundation to build teams internally that enable everyone to participate in establishing the initial phase of the journey and recruit the people who have the lived experiences and commitment to these values. As for the Equity Team itself, Watson hopes, "there should be a day when we don't need an E-Team."[45]

This day would likely be a point when a commitment to diversity, equity, and inclusion is fully embedded into the organization and its overall culture. The clarity around why the foundation is committed to these values would be unquestioned. The level of commitment would also have to be evident in external communities and among all Meyer grantees.

That day arrived in late 2018 when DePass promoted a staffer with deep experience in DEI program strategies, policy development and implementation in state government and nonprofit organizations to become Meyer's full-time internal Diversity, Equity and Inclusion Manager. Carol Cheney now oversees further efforts to operationalize equity within Meyer. With the creation of the new role, which emerged from years of work by the Equity Team, the team was dismantled. Cheney, who identifies as a queer woman of color with rural roots, reports directly to DePass and oversees a $360,000 budget.

At this point, the question is whether the foundation is better positioned now than when it started the journey to become genuinely diverse, equitable, and inclusive. It appears, the Equity Team was a valuable way to create a participatory structure to involve everyone in the process of establishing an equity journey. Watson and Lowe, in speculating about future structural changes demonstrate some of the limitations of the Equity Team model, which was not a decision-making body.

Nevertheless, it is clear that Meyer has made some strides in recent years. It committed itself to the journey and the values of diversity, equity, and inclusion, changed its composition, changed its leadership, established an effective internal structure through the Equity Team, and created various policies and practices. In considering his departure at the time of his interview in early 2018, Stamm said, "One of the reasons why I feel like it's the right time for me to leave is that I've taken it to where I can, but [equity] is embedded in this organization's DNA at this point."[46] This is a clear turning point. Not only was Stamm departing in early 2018, he was leaving with a particular perspective about the need for transition. He saw his role as bringing Meyer to a particular position. To Stamm, evidence of a commitment to equity embedded into the Trust's DNA was a signal for change – a moment to usher in a new phase along the equity journey. Now the foundation is under new leadership, and only positioned to continue the journey, as DePass brings a pre-existing dedication to these issues and was hired with this in mind. The Trustees were intentional partners in helping to continue to advance Meyer's equity journey in this hire.

It appears many pieces are in place to further facilitate Meyer's journey. For foundations, it is important to be continually mindful of how to embed the commitment even more deeply into the institution. It is always important to remember that this kind of change in philanthropy is often counter to existing paradigms and power dynamics. In speaking to these tensions, Lowe indicated a concern looking ahead. She said, "Since foundations have so much power, I am a little worried because foundations also love trends. …used to be collective impact. There are some foundations that have taken it seriously, but I worry that foundations might drastically change, but then forget to follow through and retain equity for the long-term. Doing the work meaningfully requires a lot of support. This isn't a strategy that will be a flash in the pan."[47] Indeed, there have been many trends that have passed in and out of philanthropy over the years. This is an intriguing point in philanthropic history – a time when there is more attention than ever on diversity, equity, and inclusion. This also includes particular attention to racial equity.

Institutional change in foundations, that fully integrates these principles into ideas as well as policies and practices would have to lean toward permanence to be truly effective. While there is a journey to achieve a point of greater diversity, inclusivity, and equity, there isn't necessarily and end. Lowe highlights the power of foundations. This very power could gradually push a foundation that has made progress in the other direction. This is what she wants Meyer to avoid. This is an important consideration. Ultimately, if philanthropy as a field is going to change, this change would have to be reflected in the work of particular foundations. Lessons from foundations that have progressed would have to inform behavior across the philanthropic field.

Meyer has laid the groundwork for ongoing progress on its equity journey. Their efforts have already received notoriety outside of Oregon. As a private foundation, Meyer leveraged the opportunity presented by the flexibility in their mission. Its founder did not tie the Trust's future to his descendants and even encouraged the institution's ability to evolve with the needs of the times. The change underway at Meyer continues to be driven by an increasingly diverse staff and Board. Meyer opted to change its composition as a crucial feature along their equity journey. Thus, its approach to inclusion was to bring in external voices from diverse communities with lived experiences in the foundation's priority areas. Indeed, this is more of an internally focused approach with external dimensions, by bringing the outside in. The Meyer Memorial Trust recognizes the need for a considerable amount of additional work, and appears focused on building on their progress.

Notes

1 (Meyer Memorial Trust, *Consolidated Financial Statements*, 2018)
2 (Meyer Memorial Trust, *Awards Database*, 2019)
3 (Meyer Memorial Trust, *About - Team*, 2019)
4 (Meyer Memorial Trust, *About*, 2019)
5 (Meyer Memorial Trust, *About - Mission*, 2019)
6 Ibid.
7 (Interview, Stamm 2018)
8 (Meyer Memorial Trust, *Bio of Doug Stamm*, 2019)
9 Ibid.
10 (KGW8 News 2018)
11 (Willamette Week 2018)
12 For the purposes of this book, private foundations are independent foundations that are not governed by family members. Family foundations are also private foundations, but they bring unique dynamics that are often distinct from those faced by private foundations without involved living donors or Boards comprised of mostly relatives of the donors.
13 (Interview, Stamm 2018)
14 Ibid.
15 (Meyer Memorial Trust, *About Meyer - Trustees*, 2019)
16 (National Committee for Responsive Philanthropy 2017)
17 (Meyer Memorial Trust, *About Meyer - Our Approach*, 2019)
18 Ibid.
19 Ibid.
20 Ibid.
21 Ibid.
22 (Interview, Stamm 2018)
23 (Meyer Memorial Trust, *Community - Annual Funding Opportunity*, 2019)
24 (Meyer Memorial Trust, *Education - Annual Funding Opportunity*, 2019)
25 (Meyer Memorial Trust, *Healthy Environment - Annual Funding Opportunity*, 2019)
26 (Meyer Memorial Trust, *Housing Opportunities - Annual Funding Opportunity*, 2019)
27 (Interview, Stamm 2018)
28 Ibid.
29 (Interview, Wilson 2018)

30 (Interview, Watson 2018)
31 (Interview, Lowe 2018)
32 (Interview, Stamm 2018)
33 Ibid.
34 (Interview, Watson 2018)
35 Ibid.
36 (Interview, Lowe 2018)
37 (Interview, Stamm 2018)
38 Ibid.
39 (Interview, Stamm 2018)
40 (Interview, Lowe 2018)
41 (Interview, Watson 2018)
42 Ibid.
43 (Interview, Lowe 2018)
44 (Interview, Watson 2018)
45 Ibid.
46 (Interview, Stamm 2018)
47 (Interview, Lowe 2018)

References

KGW8 News. *Meyer Memorial Trust Hires New School Dean as Next CEO*. February 8, 2018. https://www.kgw.com/article/news/meyer-memorial-trust-hires-new-school-dean-as-next-ceo/283-516215458 (accessed February 22, 2019).

Lowe, Karissa. Interview with David Maurrasse and Joey DeMarco. Video Interview Recording. New York, February 26, 2018.

Meyer Memorial Trust. *About*. 2019. https://mmt.org/about (accessed September 3, 2019).

Meyer Memorial Trust. *About Meyer – About Meyer – Our Approach*. 2019. https://mmt.org/about/our-approach (accessed February 23, 2019).

Meyer Memorial Trust. *About Meyer – Trustees*. 2019. https://mmt.org/about/trustees (accessed February 23, 2019).

Meyer Memorial Trust. *About – Mission*. 2019. https://mmt.org/about/mission (accessed September 3, 2019).

Meyer Memorial Trust. *About – Team*. 2019. https://mmt.org/about/team (accessed September 3, 2019).

Meyer Memorial Trust. *Awards Database*. 2019. https://mmt.org/awards-database (accessed September 3, 2019).

Meyer Memorial Trust. *Bio of Doug Stamm*. 2019. https://mmt.org/sites/default/files/inline-files/DougStammslongbio_0.pdf (accessed February 23, 2019).

Meyer Memorial Trust. *Community – Annual Funding Opportunity*. 2019. https://mmt.org/portfolio/community/funding-opportunities (accessed February 23, 2019).

Meyer Memorial Trust. *Consolidated Financial Statements*. 2018. https://mmt.org/sites/default/files/inline-files/CN%20Audited%20Financials%202018-0331.pdf (accessed September 3, 2019).

Meyer Memorial Trust. *Education – Annual Funding Opportunity*. 2019. https://mmt.org/portfolio/education/annual-opportunity (accessed February 23, 2019).

Meyer Memorial Trust. *Healthy Environment – Annual Funding Opportunity*. 2019. https://mmt.org/portfolio/environment/annual-opportunity (accessed February 23, 2019).

Meyer Memorial Trust. *Housing Opportunities – Annual Funding Opportunity.* 2019. https://mmt. org/portfolio/housing/annual-opportunity (accessed February 23, 2019).

National Committee for Responsive Philanthropy. *"Changing Course" Award for Incorporating Feedback: Meyer Memorial Trust.* 2017. https://www.ncrp.org/initia tives/ncrp-impact-awards/past-ncrp-impact-awards-winners/2017-ncrp-impact-awa rds-winners/meyer-memorial-trust (accessed February 20, 2019).

Stamm, Doug. Interview with David Maurrasse and Joey DeMarco. Video Interview Recording. New York, January 18, 2018.

Watson, Cristina. Interview with David Maurrasse and Joey DeMarco. Video Interview Recording. New York, February 26, 2018.

Willamette Week. Meyer Memorial Trust, Among Oregon's Largest Philanthropies, Names New CEO. February 8, 2018. https://www.wweek.com/news/city/2018/02/08/meyer-m emorial-trust-among-oregons-largest-philanthropies-names-new-ceo/ (accessed February 22, 2019).

Wilson, Kimberly. Interview with David Maurrasse and Joey DeMarco. Video Interview Recording. New York, February 26, 2018.

3

PHILANTHROPY IN EUROPE

The LankellyChase Foundation

Background on the Foundation

The LankellyChase Foundation, with approximately £140.1 million in assets,[1] based in London, U.K., was created in 2004 out of a merger between two existing foundations – The Chase Charity and the Lankelly Foundation. The Boards of these foundations decided to combine resources and create a larger entity, which could help organizations addressing "hidden or neglected forms of disadvantage or harm".[2] Women in the criminal justice system and ethnic inequality in mental health are examples of issues the new foundation would address. The organizations working on issues of this sort, in the foundation's view, were having difficulty accessing "mainstream funding".[3] Therefore, the newly formed Lankelly Chase Foundation was positioned to fill a void in local philanthropy in the United Kingdom.

Over time, the foundation increasingly began to reflect on its role and impact, leading to a more systemic understanding of the various aspects of disadvantage the foundation prioritized. In 2011, the foundation began to reframe its strategic direction and increasingly engage grantee organizations and the communities they work alongside to improve Lankelly Chase's understanding of the complexity of circumstances that shape disadvantages. As Lankelly Chase learned from partners in various communities across the U.K., they deeply reflected on their own approach to grantmaking and their overall structure as a philanthropic institution. Consequently, Lankelly Chase ultimately abandoned the traditional definition of funding programs. While the foundation began to shift its approach upon its merger and prioritize organizations that were not being adequately supported by philanthropy, they were still structured somewhat traditionally – with funding programs and oversight from committees of their Board.

Lankelly Chase of today is an *Action Inquiry Organization*. In this new approach, Lankelly Chase is more of a collaborator with networks of partners in certain communities across the United Kingdom. The foundation's CEO, Julian Corner, described the change that happened in 2011 as follows, "We scrapped funding silos and focused on interconnectedness. We established a grants program with a pool of people we were funding – a network of organizations to be funded long term."[4] Corner arrived at the foundation in 2011, and became an important catalyst for the foundation's gradual transformation. Cathy Stancer, a director at the foundation has been at Lankelly Chase for 12 years. She reflected on how the foundation operated before and after Corner's arrival. She said, "It was very traditional when I arrived. We gave small grants without a driving strategy. We were not thinking strategically. When Julian joined us, things changed."[5]

Lankelly Chase is a foundation that is in the process of altering much of the way it conducts business as a philanthropic institution. It has changed the balance of decision-making regarding grantmaking. In fact, grantmaking, whilst a core lever for supporting change, is not the centerpiece of their work. Learning from communities is at the basis of their evolving approach. The foundation is engaging communities over time, through inquiry that can lead to action. The foundation has shed many aspects of the language associated with traditional philanthropy – referring to "grantees" as "partners" and departing from "grant programs". Programs don't drive the foundation's investments. Certain community partners in various cities throughout the United Kingdom are collaborating with the foundation to build networks, identify priority concerns, and develop actions that the foundation can support in some way.

Considerations for U.K. Philanthropy

The United Kingdom has numerous "charities", which are complemented by and composed of philanthropic institutions. A "charity" is what would be called, "nonprofit" in the U.S., as there is no legal designation in the U.K. equivalent to the tax-exempt status granted by the United States' Internal Revenue Service to "nonprofits".[6] While the United States has the most substantial nonprofit sector, it is not the only part of the developed world with a significant field of organizations that are intended to represent civil society. Additionally, significant growth in philanthropy and the nonprofit sector is not merely a U.S. phenomenon. In 2018, according to the regulators' latest available numbers, there are around 168,186 registered charities in England and Wales with total annual income of £77.4 bn[7] plus another 24,666 in Scotland.[8] In 2017, the total amount given to charity increased to £10.3 billion – however, this is driven by fewer people giving more.[9] In 2016/2017, total grant-making via different kinds of charitable foundations is estimated to be £6.5 bn.[10] In 2017, 75% of the largest single donations recorded were in the first five years.[11] £1.83 bn donated in 2016 of 310 donations, and £15 bn donated from 2007 to 2016 with 2,416 donations.[12]

As in the United States, the resources of the wealthy have been growing, and philanthropy has been expanding alongside this expansion in wealth. Britain's wealthy are giving at higher amounts than before. However, they are giving away smaller percentages of their wealth. Therefore, philanthropy is not growing at the same pace as wealth in Britain.[13] Foundations contribute a substantial portion of charitable giving. As in the U.S. and elsewhere, foundations in the U.K. come in various shapes and sizes. In 2016/2017, the U.K.'s top 300 foundations gave £3.3 billion of the £20.7 billion in total private giving, including foundations and others. The giving of these foundations represents two-fifths of the total grant spending of all charitable foundations, estimated at £6.5 billion. But, despite this enormous contribution, foundation spending is actually relatively small in comparison to government spending, which is £762 billion.[14]

Giving is more significant in the U.S. compared to the situation in U.K. from various perspectives such as giving levels (in percentage of GDP and household income), participation rates, etc. While the causes of giving in the U.S. mainly focus on religion, education and human services, philanthropy in U.K. is more relevant to medical research, international aid, and welfare.[15]

Philanthropy in the European Union is significant as well.[16] Northern and Western Europe are known for policy environments favorable to philanthropy and some degrees of organizational freedom and civic participation. As in the U.K., government funding for charitable organizations is significant. Philanthropy is deeply rooted in the culture of many European societies, where various forms of philanthropy are increasing, such as individual giving, venture philanthropy, and social investment.

Characteristics of modern philanthropy in the U.K. can be found as far back as the mid-1500s, including the emergence of secular concerns about poverty and the social issues of the day to replace the medieval concept of almsgiving. Closer to the present, the development of the welfare state post World War II, including the introduction of the NHS in 1948 stimulated debate about the relevance and role of philanthropy in comparison to government. The notion of campaigning in the 1960s and 1970s placed an emphasis on the importance of advocacy within the welfare state – a role which fell to charitable organizations. The 1980s gave rise to tax incentives for cash donations from the general public, encouraging mass participation in charitable giving.[17] We can see that the welfare state coexists with a growing charitable sector in the U.K., encouraged by government. The discussion about the very role of philanthropy in comparison to government is quite robust at the LankellyChase Foundation. In the U.S., the concept of "big government" is frowned upon significantly in some settings. But there is also concern about the idea of philanthropy attempting to fulfill roles that government should play in the U.S.

The growth in U.K. giving in recent years represents a renewal of interest in philanthropy, as foundation giving declined in the immediate aftermath of the 2008 financial crisis.[18] With strong financial growth in 2016/17, foundations increased their total spending by 8.2%, and 63% of individual foundations saw a real increase in grant-making.[19] A few other factors contributed to increases in giving, such as the rise in the availability of philanthropic advice, growing media attention on philanthropy, efforts such as the Giving Pledge that encourage holding most of one's wealth aside for philanthropic giving, offers to match gifts from government and other institutions, and other variables.[20] Some growth in grant-making is fueled by new gifts to existing foundations as well as newer foundations focused on particular themes and programs.[21]

Causes receiving support in the U.K. include: education/training–24%; health–11%; arts/agriculture–11%; welfare–9%, children/youth–8%; development/housing–5%.[22]

Community-focused foundations are not as prevalent in the U.K.: 59 in 2010, and 65 in 2014.[23]

Additionally, these foundations tend to be relatively small, particularly in comparison to those in the Top 300.

At £2.02 billion, *personal and family philanthropy* accounts for 62% of the total value of Top 300 grant-making, growing by 10.2%; *corporate foundations* account for 7%, which is £2.02 million. Fluctuations in the outlook of founding companies often account for volatility in asset growth.[24] While community-focused foundations are not plentiful, a number of the larger foundations are pursuing place-focused strategies. Some new initiatives are collaborative efforts among foundations to combine resources in order to benefit local communities, to find more holistic and sustainable solutions to local issues.[25] This is the approach consistent with Lankelly Chase's method. It is not the tradition of most existing U.K. foundations, but there is some emergence of new thinking that resonates with Lankelly Chase's perspective.

When comparing U.K. foundation policy, practice, and research discourses with those in Germany and the United States, it is clear that the diverse foundation forms, approaches, and distinctions within the German and U.S. landscapes resonate with a variety of organizations in the U.K.'s nonprofit and public sectors. Yet in the U.K. most of these are currently not considered to constitute foundations – emphasis is placed on the grantmaking form.[26]

There are ongoing tensions in the U.K. between political traditions of mutuality and reciprocity on the one hand, and the governmental vision of rolling back the state with an expectation that the charity sector will fill the resulting gaps on the other.[27] As noted, this is not entirely distinct from realities in the U.S. As the nonprofit sector (or charitable sector in the case of the U.K.) continues to grow, it is likely that questions will continue regarding the respective roles of nonprofits, foundations, and donors on the one hand and the government on the other.

It is important to recognize the current climate in the U.K. regarding Brexit. In a recent series of commentaries on "Foundations and Brexit," foundation representatives highlight some of the wider effects this is likely to have on the diversity of, and approach to, their funding: funding for science, research, culture, and the environment will need to be weighed up against addressing poverty, inequality, and basic public services.[28]

Unlike in most European countries,[29] the U.K. does not provide a specific legal definition of a "charitable foundation". Concepts such as "foundation" or "trust" connote "charities with private, independent and sustainable income that fulfil their purposes by funding or otherwise supporting individuals or other organisations".[30] Consequently, it is difficult to obtain official data on foundations in the U.K. Much of the available data on foundations comes from the National Council for Voluntary Organisations (NCVO), an umbrella association for the voluntary and community sector in England.[31] Another important association is the Association of Charitable Foundations (ACF), which has over 300 members including many large independent foundations; local and community trusts; family trusts; corporate foundations; and broadcasting appeals.

There is some degree of a philanthropic industry in the U.K., but it is quite small in comparison to the many 1960s associations in the U.S. The challenge for this smaller group of independent charitable foundations, which is about 0.4% of government expenditure in the U.K. is to leverage some degree of private wealth to benefit the public.[32] This is indeed the intent of Lankelly Chase. This foundation exists within a context of a small but growing charitable sector amidst continuous tension regarding the relative responsibility of the state. This is significant considering the role of philanthropy in society in the U.K. There is growing wealth and growing charitable giving, along with growing expectation in the face of government anticipation of an expanded role for the charitable sector in addressing some of the most pressing issues facing U.K. communities. This dynamic is exacerbated by the emergence and future of Brexit. In this context, Lankelly Chase is challenging itself to maximize impact, as well as strengthen lines of communication with communities in parts of the U.K. A part of this journey is an institutional transformation that departs from some philanthropic traditions.

Strategy – The Essence of the Foundation's Strategy

The idea of an *Action Inquiry Organization* is fundamental to Lankelly Chase's strategy. This strategy is predominantly place-based and heavily reliant on trust in organizations based in particular places. The core of their strategy is not a predetermined outline of intentions regarding particular issue areas. It is less about programs and more focused on networks of organizations and people. Corner stated, "The action inquiries are homing in on place-based work. We build networks of people who want to work differently – resilient networks of people. We seek nodal points in a system. Everything is so focused on delivery that organizations cannot focus on the interconnections."[33]

A few significant components are apparent in the way Corner and the foundation have been designing their approach. They are emphasizing communities, first and foremost. This strategy places the initiation of programmatic work in the communities the foundation serves. The action inquiry method enables the dialogue and collaboration that can help surface the full complexity of challenges confronting communities. This is not about singular issues; it emphasizes multiple issues that converge and shape the nature of how people in particular places live their lives. Their experiences are shaped by the interconnections across issues. While many foundations tend to focus on single issues in particular programs, Lankelly Chase is pursuing a different course. It is also important to note that this approach acknowledges that behaviors would have to change in order to be able to adequately address complex problems in localities. Through inquiry, they are seeking to identify not only the challenge at hand, but also the nature of the actions that would be required. Organizations would have to work differently as singular institutions and in collaboration with others in order to improve the systems that inform and define decisions, inequities, disadvantages, and other dynamics.

Central to Lankelly Chase's action inquiry-based strategy is, what the foundation calls, "system behaviors". Spending time in communities with a willingness to learn through engaging organizations and networks has helped the foundation identify common themes from place to place. Carrina Gaffney of Lankelly Chase said, "We have nine system behaviors – what people told us need to be present in order for a community to flourish."[34] They are focused on "perspective, power, and participation".[35] They are as follows:

- *Perspective*

  a   *People view themselves as a part of an interconnected whole*
  b   *People are viewed as resourceful and bringing strengths*
  c   *People share a vision*

- *Power*

  a   *Power is shared, and equality of voice actively promoted*
  b   *Decision-making is devolved*
  c   *Accountability is mutual*

- *Participation*

  a   *Open trusting relationships enable effective dialogue*
  b   *Leadership is collaborative and promoted at every level*
  c   *Feedback and collective learning drive adaptation* [36]

The first of these categories, "Perspective" emphasizes the people in communities. It views people in communities as assets with knowledge and strengths to share. This is an important ongoing conversation in philanthropy regarding the role of communities that receive grants. Communities that have been historically underserved, for Lankelly Chase are viewed through their lenses rather than the foundation's. Additionally, these system behaviors are aspirational. The foundation is observing how residents and community-based organizations view their surroundings and understand the ecosystem of interactions and decisions around them. The reference to "an interconnected whole" suggests that partners in communities aspire to a point in which they view their neighborhood, city, and region as a multifaceted system. This is beyond the singular program emphasis from which Lankelly Chase is departing. Furthermore, the foundation is being informed by people in a given community who share a vision for the improvements they would like to see. Therefore, the foundation's perspective on the complexities that converge in these communities is shaped by the lived experiences of those residing in these geographic places. None of these conditions – seeing interconnectedness, recognizing community and individual resources and strengths, and sharing a vision – are automatic in any community or even within an organization.

The second category, "Power" addresses system behaviors that might be the most challenging to achieve. The ideas of sharing power, devolving decision making, and sharing accountability are contrary to the ways in which most communities and organizations are arranged. Lankelly Chase is presenting a challenge to its partner communities, but given traditional interactions between foundations and grantees/constituents, a challenge to themselves as well. This set of system behaviors requires a radical shift in culture. In a given community, if these behaviors are achieved, much of the status quo would be altered. The third category, "Participation" is central to the notion of inclusion. Trust, collaboration, and collective learning are central to how varying voices, regardless of where they are situated in a hierarchy, can be included in shaping priorities.

Overall, the foundation is taking bold and unconventional steps by centering their strategy on these system behaviors. This approach has implications for how they engage externally and distribute resources. It requires a major shift from how traditional grantmaking is implemented. It also presents a significant challenge to the foundation regarding how it is structured as an organization, and how it makes decisions. In many ways, Lankelly Chase has willingly presented a substantial challenge to itself regarding how it conducts itself as a philanthropic institution. By no means has the foundation fully achieved where it would like to be with respect to these system behaviors in its partner communities or institutionally, but, as Stancer stated, "It's all a journey."[37] At the time of this writing, the foundation is about seven years into its new strategy. They agree that there is a long way to go on this journey. This has a lot to do with the fact that they are aiming for dramatic paradigmatic shifts in their organization and in a few communities.

Commitment to Equity and Inclusion – The Foundation's Overall Commitment to Inclusion

The foundation is committed to embarking on a journey to be more equitable and inclusive. The System Behaviors drive the foundation's strategy as well as its overall values. Important dimensions of equity and inclusion are demonstrated in the System Behaviors. Breaking down power dynamics is fundamental to a commitment to equity. Striving for full participation among equals is central to conceptions of inclusion. "Our work is radically informed by the people," Corner reflected. He continued, "We have a way of working that does not require us to stop and have a consultation. We are not just thinking about participatory grantmaking. We want to explore how to shift and extend the power base and the nature of decision making."[38]

Habiba Nabatu is an Action Inquiry Manager at Lankelly Chase. She has been at the foundation for over five years. She is responsible for helping to implement the foundation's approach to action inquiry, leading toward System Behaviors in particular localities across the U.K. She declared, "We don't want to recreate the same power systems."[39] It is evident that the foundation is very intentional in pursuit of values that transcend dominant culture. In Nabutu's work in communities, she observes existing patterns of behavior. She reflected, "Communities can take on the dominant worldviews of themselves."[40] Here again, the foundation is well aware of the extent of the journey they are seeking as they promote their System Behaviors. Nevertheless, Lankelly Chase has developed a clear set of values that are explicitly guiding their efforts.

Gaffney was attracted to Lankelly Chase because of its values. She reflected, "I was drawn to Lankelly Chase because they think systemically."[41] Lankelly Chase questions their existence as a foundation and questions the how and why of existing systems and dominant culture. Equity and inclusion are embedded in their broader worldview.

Manifestations of Commitment — Techniques and Practices

How Inclusion Informs Strategy Programmatically

The implementation of their worldview is demonstrated in the foundation's programming. As noted, the foundation has transitioned away from thematic programs and developed an Action Inquiry Approach guided by nine System Behaviors. As an Action Inquiry Manager, it is Nabatu's role to engage communities and "co-create". She outlined aspects of her responsibilities, "We get invited into communities in different ways. In some areas, we have funded an organization to do partner work. In these cases, the foundation will come in behind these organizations. In other cases, the local authority invites us in, but this would only be a starting point. We would want to have connections with people in different parts of the system."[42] She indicated that the foundation is now in five or six places. Apparently, the foundation's values are guiding their actions as they connect with people in various communities. First of all, they are invited to communities. They are not driving the initial decisions, as would often be the case in philanthropic strategy. When asked about how these initial decisions to engage particular localities is explored, Nabatu uttered, "We would not go in and initiate a process on our own. It is not our place. We want to be facilitative and supportive, but we have an opinion."[43]

The foundation's programming is based on the notion of action inquiry. This takes form in Field Action Inquiry, Knowledge Action Inquiry, Place Action Inquiry and Power Action Inquiry.[44] In these inquiries, the foundation asks about "what it might take" to change systems. The foundation's actions are intended to be informed by these inquiries. Their Knowledge Action Inquiry focuses on "severe and multiple disadvantage". The foundation has been addressing the intersection among issues such as domestic abuse, homelessness, contact with the criminal justice system and others. The suggestion is that these kinds of issues have a combined and overlapping impact on people's lives. The foundation has supported research that has increased their understanding of the intersecting impact of these issues among different populations in various U.K. communities.

Lankelly Chase's Power Action Inquiry addresses how power impacts the experiences of those with severe and multiple disadvantages. This inquiry explores manifestations of power in the relationship between foundations and funded organizations as well as the ways in which disadvantaged community residents are out of control of their futures. Power became a significant focal point in the foundation's work because they heard repeatedly about the reality of dis-empowerment in the lived experiences of communities facing substantial dis-advantages. Conversations on these dynamics are continuing with the foundation's network of partners. This is the area in which Lankelly Chase is continually identifying ways in which they can share power with their partners and their communities.

The foundation's Building the Field Action Inquiry focuses on strengthening and developing the field of system change. This effort emphasizes shifting the culture of how severe and multiple disadvantages are addressed. In this regard, Lankelly Chase is acting as a facilitator and convener in order to bring together a broad network of those with a systemic change lens to social change from across sectors, places, and fields. This is where the foundation is exploring its role as an institutional actor, beyond a grant making entity, which can leverage change through multi stakeholder collaboration. The foundation is investigating where it can connect to existing networks that are seeking to alter conventional methods and think systemically.

Their Place Action Inquiry reflects the foundation's focus on place as a way to investigate and understand systems. They wanted to focus on the places where people with severe and multiple disadvantage reside. Based on feedback they have received, Lankelly Chase is seeking to collaborate with numerous partners in a few localities in order to influence change in the systemic conditions in those places. In the places where Lankelly Chase has been engaging communities, systems are reflected in patterns of interconnections across people and institutions. This inquiry operates with the following assumptions:

- We are all part of the system.
- It's not our role to make change, we build conditions for change to flourish.
- No one person holds the whole truth.
- Everyone needs to recognise and acknowledge their own need to change.
- Systems produce outcomes, not organisations or projects.
- Everyone within such a system must have a voice about how the system works.
- Everything and everyone exists in relationships. To fully understand a person or thing, you have to understand their relationships to other things.
- Emotions are present in all of this work. We need to acknowledge and work with this.[45]

The foundation is engaging in inquiry with these assumptions in England as well as Scotland. Lankelly Chase is supporting other foundations and national agencies, particular organizations that are working collaboratively, and working directly through intermediaries. In England, the foundation is present in such communities as Barking & Dagenham, Manchester, York, Birmingham, and others. As previously noted, there is no uniform approach to the foundation's engagement from one place to the next. They are working to bring together those with lived experiences and decision makers to cocreate solutions in Manchester. In York, the work began with those consistently requiring emergency services.[46] They are taking different approaches in other places.

In Scotland, Lankelly Chase is working with a cluster of other foundations[47] to reach areas that have received little philanthropic funding. They have been making relatively small investments to enable "locally led solutions to local issues" focusing on "incremental changes".[48] This effort, "People in Place" is active in eight communities across seven local authorities – Blacklands, North Ayrshire; Buckhaven, Fife; Castlehill, West Dunbartonshire, Cumnock, East Ayrshire; Dunterlie, East Renfrewshire; Fernhill, South Lanarkshire; Langlees, Falkirk; Methil, Fife.[49] This work is expanding to other Scottish communities as well. These are areas where populations are facing significant challenges, but receiving little attention from foundations. They are listening to people in these communities in order to identify the nature of priority concerns and consider solutions. The foundations participating in this effort are looking to improve their practice based on learning from these communications. They are continuing to build partnerships across sectors in these areas.

This effort in Scotland demonstrates Lankelly Chase's collaboration with other foundations around a place-based approach that includes many of the characteristics reflected in Lankelly Chase's approach, such as listening to those with lived experiences in places in order to inform how the foundation continues work in these localities. One can also see an awareness of power dynamics among these other foundations as well, seeking to share with communities how to establish the role that foundations play in their neighborhoods and cities. Given Lankelly Chase's systemic emphasis, it is advantageous to collaborate with other foundations and combine resources. The selection of sites that have been overlooked by philanthropy is another interesting dimension of this effort. It highlights how many areas of great need do not necessarily receive philanthropic support. This effort is not only bringing new resources to these communities, it is involving these local populations in shaping solutions.

How Inclusion Informs Strategy Institutionally

Institutionally, Lankelly Chase is clearly challenging themselves to live their values, particularly system behaviors. One aspect of how the foundation's thinking influences structure is decision making. Corner said, "The Board agreed to disband grantmaking decisions – now they are made by the executive and staff, who are closer to the organizations."[50] He continued, "There is not much precedent for this in the U.K., where Trustees make the decisions. None of our Trustees are family members; the founders never wanted family members involved."[51] He makes a couple of interesting points regarding the nature of philanthropy in the U.K. as well as the involvement of family members. Lankelly Chase is departing from tradition regarding Trustee decision making, which is the norm in many U.K. foundations. He also references how the founders of the foundation did not want family members involved. Therefore, even before the shift toward system behaviors there was some sentiment regarding the role of family member decision making in philanthropy.

Indeed, there is a logic to delegating decision making to those working closer to the communities of interest to the foundation. Especially with Lankelly Chase's Action Inquiry approach, the foundation is much better positioned to be effective if the staff who are engaging constituents in various neighborhoods are making decisions about investing the foundation's funds rather than Board members. Corner has an interesting way of characterizing the shift in their process, "We replaced top down with middle down."[52] As noted, the foundation is no longer considering itself to be a "Grantmaking Foundation".

Of course, institutional change does not appear instantly. It requires changes in behavior as well as transformations in culture. Their approach requires people with the competencies and comfort level to operate from an inquiry basis, which does require giving up some of the power to which many foundation staff are accustomed. When asked about staffing, Corner reflected, "There has been some staff turnover. But I recruited good people; and we've invested heavily in them. The staff are highly collaborative, highly relational, extremely reflective – they notice nuances. Some colleagues from the old model adapted. I had to adapt myself."[53]

Stancer, whose time at the foundation predated Corner's, said of their internal changes, "It's all a journey. We are working hard to make sure all voices are heard internally. We are looking toward creating smaller working groups, and we have all had dialogue training such as deep democracy."[54] She highlights the time and effort required internally in order to embody the system behaviors they espouse. Once the foundation decides to shift internal decision making, it must also determine how this new approach will materialize in practice. They have sought training in order to facilitate democratic internal dialogue. When reflecting on bringing in outside assistance to guide their internal change processes, Corner said, "How we interpret our team's evolution is realizing that we do not have all of the necessary competencies, but we are bringing in other partners."[55] Recognition of the need for additional help is an important dimension of how a foundation navigates a significant transition.

Stancer also mentioned the work being done with the Board of Trustees. In her estimation, the Board should be diverse and even more representative of the communities the foundation supports. The current Board has eight members.[56] Five are men and three are women. All Board members appear to be white. The backgrounds of these Board members include some with lived experience of multiple disadvantages and all bring direct work experience in the kinds of communities in which the foundation is working. Changing a Board is a part of the overall aforementioned "journey".

The foundation is actively looking to diversify the Board. She indicated that the Board has been in the process of changing, "When Julian joined us, we had a Board split between those who were traditional and those who wanted to change. We have recruited new people who share our ambitions."[57] As with staffing, the foundation has been intentionally adding Board members who are a better fit given their direction. Not surprisingly, at the point of changing course, the foundation had both Board members who were more comfortable with a previous method of operating, and those who were ready for a different path.[58]

It should be noted that the U.K. is becoming more diverse. The U.K. was 92.1% white in 2001. In 2011 it was 87.2%. The next census will be in 2021. The U.K. has been experiencing noticeable increases among Asian and Black populations. The total Asian population increased from 4.4% in 2001 to 6.9% in 2011. The Black population increased from 2% in 2001 to 3% in 2011 with noticeable increases in the population of immigrants from the African continent.[59] As U.K. communities become more diverse, dialogue about diversity, equity, and inclusion will likely increase. One aspect of becoming a diverse, equitable, and inclusive institution will be greater representation of varying populations in the U.K. at all levels, and particularly representation reflective of the communities which foundations hope to impact.

Nabatu, who is of African descent, referenced "internal tensions" in the process of change at the foundation. She does notice how they are getting closer to reflecting system behaviors in their internal practice. But she sees room for improvement. "We have to let go of being in control," she said. The goal is to better demonstrate their stated intentions. She declared, "We want decisions to be made locally; we want to model system behaviors."[60] She continued, "The structure of the organization is not necessarily right. Politics, economics, people's sense of self agency, power, dominant narratives all have to be addressed. People should have agency to demand better."[61] Nabatu sees the direct correlation between how the foundation makes decisions and how they can be a catalyst for greater agency at the community level. The prevailing systems and power dynamics that she sees in the communities where she is working as an Action Inquiry Manager are reflected in foundations themselves, as institutions. The structure that would best enable a substantially different method of operating in communities must exemplify system behaviors. Given that most foundations are not structured in this manner, there is little precedent for this thinking, and more significantly, putting these ideas into practice.

Progress and Learning

Measuring progress in philanthropy is never simple. Even when programs are reduced to highly specified outcomes, the full range of impact of a particular grant is typically not captured. The approach that Lankelly Chase is pursuing is not conducive to short term outcomes. Furthermore, the foundation's emphasis on complexity and interconnectedness is harder to quantify than a few distinct outcomes. Nabatu sees progress in the foundation's commitment to a new set of values, but encourages even further departure from traditional conceptions of evaluation in philanthropy. She declared, "The foundation has gotten much better at articulating our vision and role." She continued, referring to broader dynamics in philanthropic culture and practice, "We have to get rid of outcomes and projects and value learning."[62]

This emphasis on learning is quite conducive to the action inquiry approach they have selected. It is centered on learning by engaging constituents in various localities to help understand and address prevailing systems. The foundation's vision is the manifestation of a range of system behaviors in various U.K. communities, and beyond, including in philanthropy. Measuring progress in this regard is an inherently longer-term endeavor than most philanthropic evaluation or assessment projects. The foundation recognizes the importance of progress toward system behaviors incrementally, which includes the foundation's own progress in modeling the behavior it hopes to stimulate across the U.K.

Indeed, the most apparent impact of Lankelly Chase's relatively emerging approach is learning. Learning influences the nature and scope of their efforts in U.K. communities. It has also influenced the foundation's own behavior. Corner indicated, "We created a learning community of organizations with unrestricted funds to take the work where it needed to go."[63] He added, "Our learning from these organizations affected the foundation. We began to observe effective organizations have common characteristics – which are the system behaviors."[64] Both the foundation's commitment to transform internally, and its adoption of system behaviors were directly influenced by their learning from community organizations. Consequently, the outcomes of the foundation's community engagement are already significant. If the foundation and their partners are able to demonstrably alter system behaviors in a number of U.K. communities, their impact will be somewhat dramatic.

The kinds of issues that many foundations address in their programming – what Lankelly Chase sees as severe and multiple disadvantages – cannot be solved with short term and piecemeal projects. Lankelly Chase's engagement in local communities underscored the need for broader collaborative efforts targeting intersections. The foundation began to act accordingly, clarifying the specific system behaviors that could reorient the persistence of disadvantages. Therefore, if the foundation's efforts can help transform existing paradigms in communities that will lead to system behaviors, systems change will occur. First, this level of change would occur at the community level. But lessons from these changes could influence many other places. Ultimately, if additional foundations find success in bringing about systems change, a multiplier effect might ensue. Lankelly Chase has committed itself to a journey that is comprehensive, complex, and likely daunting. They realize that continued progress will require additional engagement and learning.

Direction and Conclusions

While philanthropy has been undergoing growth in the U.K., overall, this is a time of uncertainty due to Brexit. This current period is on the heels of a time of austerity, which impacted the development and application of philanthropy. Comer reflected on the evolution of philanthropy in the U.K. in recent years. He said, "The U.K. has had a sustained era of austerity. Philanthropy has taken different approaches during this period. One approach was additionality – fund efforts that are outside of State control. There is also an approach to fund things the State should support, and hope it will be mainstreamed. But there is no money for this. The era of initiatives becoming national programs is over. But there is a growing sense of the importance of place."[65] Clearly, Lankelly Chase's experiences are somewhat parallel to this trend of emphasizing place. The great disadvantages that Lankelly Chase seeks to address are manifested in places. Although the foundation's approach of deepening engagement in place by way of inquiry, rather than deciding on priorities followed by grants, is not a dominant trend in philanthropy.

In the Brexit era, Comer notices that communities that have been overlooked tended to vote for Brexit. Geographic areas of great need that have not benefited from adequate investment are now receiving greater attention. Comer indicated, "We now have 360 Giving, which tells us where the money goes, which highlighted that parts of the country are not getting much funding. They are often referred to as 'Left Behind Communities' – smaller de-industrialized towns."[66] Looking forward for philanthropy in the U.K., it will be important for foundations to attain a better sense of community needs, and act accordingly. Comer declared, "Foundations do not have good antennae for understanding the needs of communities."[67] Lankelly Chase has been attempting to transcend these philanthropic blind spots by going directly to communities of significant need in order to understand the needs of local populations and how often systems work to perpetuate disadvantages.

This is not a quick process. Consequently, the future of Lankelly Chase's work is grounded in continuous engagement and inquiry. It is not a matter of a brief, focused grant making strategy. This is a matter of ongoing partnership between the foundation and stakeholders in select local communities. Looking ahead, Stancer said, "We are working hard on structuring learning." She continued, "We have learning partners independent of the foundation helping us learn and get a sense of what is happening."[68] Continuity is embedded in the foundation's method. Therefore, consistency over several years, rather than shorter-term grants in one or two years, is the basis of their philanthropic strategy. Corner, indicated, "We presume a grant over three years is not enough. We want to continue to ask, 'So what? What is showing up in the work?'"[69]

A place-based approach including continuous partnership and inquiry provides Lankelly Chase the opportunity to understand how multiple issues intersect and how an ecosystem of actors in a community affects how issues influence the livelihoods of, particularly, disadvantaged populations. Systems shape the life chances of residents in their places. From the foundation's perspective, one cannot readily understand these systems without inquiry and sustained engagement that can only be possible after trust is established over time. As Gaffney says, "We need to think about the interconnected whole."[70] These interconnections are complex, and not readily apparent to outsiders. Furthermore, insiders in communities may not be ready to address the full nature of interconnecting issues right away. As has been noted, power dynamics are often deeply embedded in communities. Change will not simply materialize without the time to collectively diagnose the nature of the challenge. Nabatu thinks the foundation should continue to inquire about change. "How do we as individuals in the foundation really think change happens?" she wondered.[71] Chances are the foundation will continue to learn about viable pathways to change in the communities in which they are working. They will also learn much more about barriers to change as well. According to Gaffney, all of this learning is relevant, and should be shared. She said, "We need to share what we learn as much as possible, especially where we make mistakes."[72]

The way in which Lankelly Chase has been questioning philanthropy and the very nature of foundations is intriguing. This is an area where it is clear how agreeing on a set of values, or in this instance, system behaviors, has helped shape inquiry on many levels, including the very role of philanthropic dollars. Nabatu pondered, "What's our theory of money? What can our money get us?"[73] These are rather fundamental questions that are indicative of how Lankelly Chase has been challenging themselves and philanthropy in general. Their inquiries and system behaviors are seeking mutual transformation – in the communities in which they are working and in the foundation itself. The "journey" that Lankelly Chase's stakeholders referenced is multifaceted. It appears the foundation is committed to continuing on a path of sustained learning. This learning will drive their philanthropic strategy to ultimately influence change in particular U.K. communities.

Notes

1 (The LankellyChase Foundation, *Annual Report*, 2018)
2 (The LankellyChase Foundation, *About Us*, 2019)
3 Ibid.
4 (Interview, Corner 2018)
5 (Interview, Stancer 2019)
6 (Janus n.d.)
7 (Charity Commission for England and Wales 2019)
8 (Scottish Charity Regulator 2019)
9 (Charities Aid Foundation 2018)
10 (Pharoah et al. 2019)
11 (Coutts Institute 2017)
12 Ibid.
13 (Stead n.d.)
14 (Pharoah et al. 2019)
15 (Wright 2001)
16 (Observatoire de la Fondation de France 2015)
17 (Davies 2016)
18 (Pharoah et al. 2016)
19 (Pharoah et al. 2019)
20 (Coutts Institute 2017)
21 (Pharoah et al. 2019)
22 (Pharoah et al. 2016)
23 (Kilmurray and Hodgson 2015)
24 Ibid.
25 Ibid.
26 (Jung 2018)
27 Ibid.
28 Ibid.
29 (McGill 2016)
30 (Association of Charitable Foundations 2019)
31 (McGill 2016)
32 (Association of Charitable Foundations 2019)
33 (Interview, Corner 2018)
34 (Interview, Gaffney 2019)
35 (The LankellyChase Foundation, *Our Approaches – System Behaviours* 2019)
36 Ibid.
37 (Interview, Stancer 2019)
38 (Interview, Corner 2018)
39 (Interview, Nabatu 2019)
40 Ibid.
41 (Interview, Gaffney 2019)
42 (Interview, Nabatu 2019)

43 Ibid.
44 (The LankellyChase Foundation, *Our Work*, 2019)
45 (The LankellyChase Foundation, *Our Work – Place*, 2019)
46 (The LankellyChase Foundation, *Our Work – Place – England*, 2019)
47 The foundations involved in People in Place are Lankelly Chase, Esmée Fairbairn Foundation, Joseph Rowntree Foundation, the Tudor Trust and Corra Foundation
48 (The LankellyChase Foundation, *Our Work – Place – Scotland*, 2019)
49 Ibid.
50 (Interview, Corner 2018)
51 Ibid.
52 Ibid.
53 Ibid.
54 (Interview, Stancer 2018)
55 (Interview, Corner 2018)
56 (The LankellyChase Foundation, *About Us - Trustees*, 2019)
57 (Interview, Stancer 2018)
58 (Interview, Nabatu 2019)
59 (Office for National Statistics, UK 2011)
60 Ibid.
61 Ibid.
62 (Interview, Nabatu 2019)
63 (Interview, Corner 2018)
64 Ibid.
65 Ibid.
66 Ibid.
67 Ibid.
68 (Interview, Stancer 2018)
69 (Interview, Corner 2018)
70 (Interview, Gaffney 2019)
71 (Interview, Nabatu 2019)
72 (Interview, Gaffney 2019)
73 (Interview, Nabatu 2019)

References

Association of Charitable Foundations. *What is a Foundation?*2019. https://www.acf.org. U.K./about/what-is-a-foundation/ (accessed May 21, 2019).

Charities Aid Foundation. *UK Giving Report 2018*. 2018. https://www.cafonline.org/docs/default-source/about-us-publications/caf-U.K.-giving-2018-report.pdf (accessed May 15, 2019).

Charity Commission for England and Wales. *Charity Register Statistics*. 2019. https://www.gov.U.K./government/publications/charity-register-statistics/recent-charity-register-statistics-charity-commission (accessed May 20, 2019)

Corner, Julian. Interview with David Maurrasse. Telephone Recording. New York, August 3, 2018.

Coutts Institute. *Million Pound Donors Report 2017 Celebrating and Inspiring Philanthropy*. 2017. https://www.coutts.com/insight-articles/news/2017/million-pound-donors-report-2017.html?extcam=donorsreport (accessed May 18, 2019).

Davies, Rhodri. *A Timeline of Modern British Philanthropy*. 2016. https://www.cafonline.org/about-us/blog-home/giving-thought/the-role-of-giving/a-timeline-of-modern-british-philanthropy (accessed May 18, 2019).

Gaffney, Carrina. Interview with David Maurrasse and Michele Favero. Video Interview Recording. New York, May 13, 2019.

Janus, Lauren. *Thoughtful Philanthropy: Three Stand-out Differences Between Nonprofits in the US and UK*, N.d. https://www.thoughtfulphilanthropy.com/three-stand-differ ences-nonprofits-us-U.K./ (accessed May 14, 2019).

Jung, Tobias. Foundations in the UK: Organizations and nations in a state of flux. *American Behavioral Scientist* 62, no. 13. 2018. https://www.dropbox.com/s/smmk84iaisgh1et/ Foundations%20in%20the%20U.K..pdf?dl=0 (accessed May 20, 2019).

Kilmurray, Avila and Jenny Hodgson. *Community Philanthropy: The Context, Concepts, and Challenges: A Literature Review*. 2015. http://www.globalfundcommunityfoundations. org/information/community-philanthropy-the-context-concepts-and-challenges-a.html (accessed May 19, 2019).

McGill, T. Lawrence. European Foundation Sector Report 2016: Number of registered public benefit foundations in Europe exceeds 147,000. *Foundation Center (New York) Report*. 2016. https://www.issuelab.org/resource/european-foundation-sector-report-2016-num ber-of-registered-public-benefit-foundations-in-europe-exceeds-147-000.html (accessed May 21, 2019).

Nabatu, Habiba. Interview with David Maurrasse and Michele Favero. Video Interview Recording. New York, May 13, 2019.

Observatoire de la Fondation de France. *An Overview of Philanthropy in Europe*. 2015. http://fdnweb.org/ffdf/files/2014/09/philanthropy-in-europe-overview-2015-report. pdff (accessed May 18, 2019).

Office for National Statistics, UK. *Ethnicity and National Identity in England and Wales*. 2011. https://www.ethnicity-facts-figures.service.gov.U.K./U.K.-population-by-ethnicity/nat ional-and-regional-populations/population-of-england-and-wales/latest (accessed May 20, 2019).

Pharoah, Cathy, Richard Jenkins, Keiran Goddard, Catherine Walker. *Giving Trends: Top 300 Foundation Grand-Makers 2016 Report*. 2016. https://www.acf.org.U.K./downloa ds/publications/ACF123_Foundation_Giving_Trends_2016_Design_AW_Web_pgs.pdf (accessed May 19, 2019).

Pharoah. Cathy, Catherine Walker, Emma Hutchins. *Giving Trends: Top 300 Foundation Grand-Makers 2018 Report*. 2019. https://www.acf.org.U.K./downloads/publications/ ACF147_Foundation_Giving_Trends_2018_For_web_spreads.pdf (accessed May 15, 2019).

Scottish Charity Regulator. *Homepage*. 2019. https://www.oscr.org.U.K./ (accessed May 15, 2019).

Stancer, Cathy. Interview with David Maurrasse and Michele Favero. Video Interview Recording. New York, May 13, 2019.

Stead, David. *UK and International Trends in Philanthropy*. N.d. http://philanthropy-impact. org/expert-opinion/U.K.-and-international-trends-philanthropy (accessed May 18, 2019).

Wright, Karen. Generosity vs. altruism: Philanthropy and charity in the United States and United Kingdom. *Voluntas: International Journal of Voluntary and Nonprofit Organizations*, 12(4), 399–416. 2001. https://cdn.ymaws.com/www.istr.org/resource/resmgr/work ing_papers_dublin/wright.pdf (accessed May 18, 2019).

The LankellyChase Foundation. *Annual Report and Financial Statements*. 2018. https://la nkellychase.org.U.K./wp-content/uploads/2018/11/Annual-Report-and-Accounts-31- Mar-2018.pdf (accessed May 15, 2019).

The LankellyChase Foundation. *About Us*. 2019. https://lankellychase.org.U.K./about-us/ (accessed May 14, 2019).

The LankellyChase Foundation. *Our Approaches – System Behaviours*. 2019. https://lankel lychase.org.U.K./our-approach/system-behaviours/ (accessed May 14, 2019).

The LankellyChase Foundation. *Our Work – Place*. 2019. https://lankellychase.org.U.K./our-work/place/ (accessed May 14, 2019).

The LankellyChase Foundation. *Our Work*. 2019. https://lankellychase.org.U.K./our-work/ (accessed May 14, 2019).

The LankellyChase Foundation. *Our Work – Place – England*. 2019. https://lankellychase.org.U.K./our-work/place/england (accessed May 14, 2019).

The LankellyChase Foundation. *Our Work – Place – Scotland*. 2019. https://lankellychase.org.U.K./our-work/place/scotland (accessed May 14, 2019).

The LankellyChase Foundation. *About Us – Trustees*. 2019. https://lankellychase.org.U.K./about-us/#trustees (accessed May 14, 2019).

4

COMMUNITY FOUNDATIONS

San Francisco Foundation

Background on the San Francisco Foundation

Founded in 1948, the San Francisco Foundation (TSFF) is a community foundation, which serves the Bay Area region of California. This area includes San Francisco, along with Marin, Contra Costa, San Mateo, and Alameda. Like most community foundations, the San Francisco Foundation includes multiple funds. Today, the foundation is situated within an economically booming region, which was the engine of a technological revolution that changed the world. While these dynamics produced great wealth, they created unprecedented inequality.

Many decades ago, when the foundation was forged by a grant from the Columbia Foundation, the intention was to create a philanthropic organization that would be "contemporary" and "sensitive to current social needs".[1] Now, as one of the larger community foundations in existence, the foundation is confronted with being relevant in its current historical context. It is faced with addressing pressing issues facing vulnerable populations in their region challenged to survive in an increasingly unaffordable reality.

With assets of US$1.4 billion and an $800 million endowment, and grantmaking of $11.5 million in 2017, the San Francisco Foundation has become an engine with great potential. According to the foundation's annual report figure,[2] $60.9 million out of the total $86.6 million giving are invested in the bay area in partnerships with the foundation's donors and there are 1,637 organizations supported by the foundation and its donors. In terms of the investment areas, the largest proportion of investment ($17 million) is for strengthening neighborhoods, leaders and collaboratives; second largest investment area is education ($15 million), followed by arts and culture as the third largest investment area.

As has been stated clearly, the foundation's mission is to "mobilize resources and act as a catalyst for change to build strong communities, foster civic leadership, and promote philanthropy".[3] To achieve its mission, the foundation is "committed to a bold equity agenda that advances greater racial and economic inclusion for everyone in the Bay Area".[4] Furthermore, the foundation decided, informed by the perspectives of communities throughout their region, to emphasize equity in their core strategy.

Considerations for Community Foundations

The number of community foundations continues to grow. There were 789[5] community foundations in the United States in 2014 and this number has increased by 14% in the last ten years. There are over 1,800 community foundations around the world. Why this expansion? Community foundations serve particular regions. Constituents within a particular geographic region, through a community foundation, can organize philanthropy designed to improve their area. In a community foundation, donors can find a home for their charitable giving while attaining expert guidance. For a particular locale, a community foundation can be a representative voice, which convenes local leaders around major issues and even advocates on behalf of the community. A community foundation can be an anchor institution – an enduring local asset that plays a vital role in its community and local economy.

Community foundations have been in existence for over 100 years. The Cleveland Foundation was the very first of its kind when it was established in 1914. Consider the breadth of change that has taken place in over 10 years. Even the San Francisco Foundation has endured for over 70 years. Economies change; demographics change; but these community foundations remain with missions dedicated to improving their localities. One important challenge in this regard is the ability to adapt to change and remain as relevant as possible given contemporary priorities.

Community foundations must balance meeting the specific needs of donors, which have established funds at the foundation with taking leadership around particular concerns within their geographic area of emphasis. As communities increasingly expect greater involvement of the nonprofit sector in addressing many basic human concerns (health, education, etc.), community foundations are uniquely positioned to invest in the organizations in their regions that are actively focusing on the priority needs of the day.

Many constituents or stakeholders with vested interests surround community foundations. Donors stand out among them, as the growth of community foundations has been fueled by the expansion of Donor Advised Funds (DAFs), which allow donors to invest funds with charitable intentions at community foundations, which they can advise. This is an alternative to a donor establishing an entirely new foundation and dealing with all of the complexities of an organization. DAFs enable community foundations to handle administration, freeing donors from these responsibilities, while leaving in place the ability to inform grantmaking from these funds. Community foundations invest and grow these funds over time. Donors can continue to make deposits into these funds to accelerate growth.

Community foundations have developed services for donors, which inform them about grantmaking, trends in their area, and connect them to a wide range of other educational and human resources. Indeed, donors have needs that community foundations are happy to meet. But low-income residents in a region and the most adversely impacted populations in a locality have needs as well. Sometimes these needs converge naturally, as donors often share substantive interests with the core purposes of a community foundation. Community foundations are challenged to reach the most vulnerable populations. Grants from the central fund of a community foundation typically support nonprofit organizations serving the region in question. However, these organizations are entities within themselves, not necessarily reflective of the perspectives of the populations they serve. Therefore, an inclusive community foundation is one that listens to a collection of stakeholders, but with particular attention to populations most adversely impacted in their region.

This includes external and internal considerations. Externally, community foundations must make themselves visible to their communities and provide opportunities to hear from these voices. Internally, community foundations have to consider being reflective of the populations they serve on the Board and staff, among donors, vendors and others interfacing with the institution. Some older community foundations are learning to adapt to newer populations in their regions. Many localities and regions in the United States and around the world are more demographically diverse. Given their need to stay relevant, community foundations, in order to be effective, must remain connected to populations in their regions. This calls for full inclusion at all levels externally and internally.

Community foundations have entered their second century of existence, which calls for reflection on the model and approach of these public charities.[6] Organizations such as CF Leads: Community Foundations Leading Change are emphasizing "community leadership" among community foundations.[7] This organization is a network of community foundations that promotes the role these institutions can play in building stronger communities. The San Francisco Foundation is an active participant in this network. The Foundation's recently developed strategy and approach reflects a commitment to building a stronger Bay Area. It also makes clear a set of values – a dedication to equity. In order for the foundation to be genuinely committed to equity and to strengthening its community by addressing the most pressing concerns facing the region, it would have to be inclusive of the varying populations in the area with particular attention to the most vulnerable among them.

The Essence of the San Francisco Foundation's Strategy

The San Francisco Foundation encapsulates their strategy in three words, "People, Place, Power". This strategy is less of a written plan and more of a set of core values to drive the nature of the foundation's work, and a somewhat new way of doing business for them. Goals in these three areas include:

People: Expanding access to opportunity through removing systemic barriers
Place: Anchoring communities to help people feel deeply rooted and connected
Power: Nurturing equity movements to ensure a strong political voice for all[8]

The strategy evolved out of the initial efforts of the foundation's President, Fred Blackwell, who arrived with a desire to get a better understanding of how the foundation could serve its target communities. Blackwell arrived at the foundation in 2014, leaving a position in local government in the Bay Area. He was Interim City Administrator for the City of Oakland. As a native of Oakland, Blackwell is from the San Francisco Foundation's region of emphasis. Upon joining the foundation, Blackwell was already interested in the community foundation model and the social justice history of the San Francisco Foundation. Of community foundations, Blackwell indicated, "Community foundations are unique. There are few places in society where there is a vast amount of types of people coming through the door on any given day."[9] For Blackwell, the foundation's work is on three levels, "Grantmaking, Facilitation of the Philanthropy above it, and Civic Leadership. Those things together allow this foundation to achieve results".[10]

It is clear that Blackwell's view considers the multifaceted dimensions inherent in the community foundation structure in considering the foundation's strategy implementation. Community foundations make grants, but they raise money from local constituents as well. Community foundations are not only institutions that make charitable contributions. They are local assets, which have can bring voice to concerns in their communities. The notion of "Civic Leadership" connotes an aspect of community foundations' efforts that suggests a significant level of engagement with local constituents and a willingness to raise awareness and influence policy and decision-making affecting the foundation's target region.

According to Foundation Board Chair, Duncan Robertson, "Fred was tremendously thoughtful about understanding the foundation and the needs of the community."[11] The Foundation's strategy, which was informed by a series of "listening sessions" held in numerous communities in the region, emphasizes regional equity. Judith Bell, the foundation's Vice President of Programs said of the regional equity strategy, "The Foundation has always had a regional footprint, but it has not had a regional agenda."[12] While the foundation's leaders recognize the institution's historical dedication to improving the region, they are essentially reshaping not only the foundation's vision and programming, they are changing the way the institution aligns all of its units around common goals. Dee Dee Brantley, the foundation's Chief Operating Officer, has been at the San Francisco Foundation for 17 years. She observed, "We are known to be steeped in social justice. It is interesting that when Fred came on board, and started embarking on an equity agenda, it was more of a pivot instead of massive changes. Really what I think has changed is we have become more focused."[13]

The Foundation is becoming more dedicated to a regional equity agenda, which includes an emphasis on racial equity. Across the foundation, this vision is referenced as a "North Star". Fred Blackwell has encouraged everyone in the foundation to understand their role in this strategic direction. Blackwell indicated, "I have a set of goals for the foundation, which everyone pastes in their offices. The goals relate to being clear about what we are doing, doing it in a way that draws on our resources and network, and seeks to achieve a greater degree of alignment between our endowment and donors."[14]

Foundation leaders have built upon the foundation's historical commitment equity and framed a vision for improving opportunities for people in the region, deepening the connection of these people to the place in which they reside, and bolstering the community's political voice in shaping the region's future. Equity is a pressing reality in a region that has become increasingly unaffordable with widening disparities. The Foundation, while historically committed to similar principles, is undergoing a transition to attempt to live up to these ideals. It is affecting the foundation in its programming and operations.

The Foundation's Commitment to Equity and Inclusion

The Foundation has been quite explicit about its commitment to equity. It is one thing to articulate a commitment, it is another to demonstrate it in action. The connection between the foundation's strategy, which emphasizes regional equity and inclusion – how the foundation includes the perspectives of its constituents in shaping the development and execution of this strategy – is an additional consideration. Like equity, inclusion is another concept that can be easily articulated without putting theory into practice. For a community foundation, with a diverse constituency representing an entire region, inclusion requires engagement with a wide range of populations.

When Blackwell arrived at the foundation, engaging the local community was a priority. With the centrality of donors to community foundations, there is a potential danger in focusing on the perspectives of donors over those of historically disenfranchised communities. A community foundation would have to take an equitable approach to inclusion in order to genuinely bring in the voices of the populations that are most adversely affected by inequities in their region.

The San Francisco Foundation has been communicating with diverse constituents through "listening" to communities. The strategic planning process included a "listening campaign". According to Blackwell, this campaign included eight neighborhood meetings of 100–200 attendees each. Blackwell said of these meetings, "We asked them to describe their neighborhood, what trends were happening, and what solutions they thought could alleviate some challenges. Each meeting had housing, education, and seniors come up. At the end of each one, people started talking about race."[15]

The strategic planning process did include engagement internal to the foundation. Some institutions do not engage beyond their internal stakeholders. The San Francisco Foundation sought to be inclusive in their strategic planning process by visiting neighborhoods in their communities and engaging constituents directly. The idea of communicating with constituents to shape strategic planning is an important step because it involves engagement at the front end of developing programs. Inclusion can take form at various stages when an institution such as a foundation engages external constituents, particularly those representing the communities served by grantees. These are often the populations that are not asked for their perspective. But they are especially overlooked early in the process before priorities are established and programs are forged.

Inclusion is relevant at various stages in strategy development – informing the establishment of strategic priorities, sharing perspectives as strategies are implemented, and reflecting on the completion of strategies. In the nonprofit sector, feedback at the back end is more commonplace. It is a significant feature in assessment and evaluation. Seeking feedback through assessment and evaluation is one dimension of inclusion. But an inclusive foundation is one that engages constituents at all stages. It is also one that considers various ways to represent populations institutionally. The San Francisco Foundation is considering all of these dimensions.

Manifestations of Commitment — Techniques and Practices

How Inclusion Informs Strategy Programmatically

The Foundation's listening campaign occurred during the strategic planning process. Blackwell found value in this campaign, and, upon reflection, would have added another. He said, "If I had to do it over again, I would have engaged another stakeholder group during the strategic development process."[16] His hope is to do more listening campaigns going forward, making them a permanent part of how they engage constituents. He declared, "I think we are overdue for another listening campaign. These should be ongoing aspects of doing the work, instead of doing it as a one-off."[17]

Community foundations have many constituents to consider in their regions. These include residents at all socioeconomic levels and representative of various demographic groups, local government, and a wide range of fields and industries. One constituent group looming large in the reality of all community foundations is donors. When the San Francisco Foundation explicitly developed a strategic plan focused on regional equity, stressing the particular significance of racial equity, donor alignment with this strategy was a concern. Ruben Orduna, the foundation's Vice President of Development and Donor Services said, regarding donor reactions to the strategic plan, "We have gotten emails from people saying they are concerned that the foundation is becoming too political, but no one has closed any funds."[18]

Donor reaction is a crucial issue when considering how a community foundation shapes its strategic direction because catering to donor intent has become integral to the business model. Community foundations have grown because of Donor Advised Funds that provide donors with significant input into the grants a community foundation makes on their behalf. The 2017 Donor-Advised Fund Report by the National Philanthropic Trust[19] analyzed data for donor-advised funds at 594 Community Foundations (CFs). The results show that in 2016 there were 69,587 individual Donor Advised Funds with charitable assets of about $29.80 billion in community foundations across the U.S. Both the number and total assets of the Donor Advised Funds at U.S. community foundations have been growing fast continuously. In 2012 there were only 60,232 Donor Advised Funds with total assets of $18.31 billion.

Judith Bell suggested the foundation is proactively trying to break down what has become a structural division within many community foundations. The central program vision of community foundations and particular attention to donors can follow two separate tracks. She said, "The history of community foundations – donor services on one side and program on the other – we are working to break this down; we have donors a part of the equity agenda. We are providing donors more opportunities to get engaged and working in partnership with donors. We are working on education on equity grantmaking with a shared pool."[20] Despite the varying interests of donors, the challenge in this circumstance is to align donors with a common vision and approach focused on equity.

Regarding donors, Fred Blackwell said, "Our role with donors is a continuum. They will be informed of the foundation's point of view; but we will also meet donors where they are."[21] This viewpoint speaks to the balancing required in engaging donors for a community foundation. On the one hand, community foundations promote a menu of donor services that meet donors' unique needs and interests. One the other, a community foundation is a mission-driven organization. Some community foundations, like the San Francisco Foundation, are prioritizing a core mission focused on pressing needs in the region. This mission is informed by, not only the foundation's Board and staff, but by the perspectives of large segments of their constituents. There is no guarantee that the interests of these constituents and those of the majority of donors will converge. In the San Francisco Foundation's case, it appears there is some alignment around an equity agenda. Blackwell added, "Three out of the last four years have been record years for fundraising."[22] For the most part, donors have been supportive of the foundation's direction. Bell indicated, "I have been pleasantly surprised by the donor response. We did a series of focus groups with donors. The donors are happy to be associated with the equity approach."[23]

The notion of inclusion is relevant on multiple levels. For a community foundation, the many stakeholders who can inform the development of program priorities can include very influential local leaders. But the most common challenge is to include the voices of those most adversely impacted – the populations that are often not asked for their perspectives around major policies or decisions. These are lower income populations, often those served by nonprofit organizations. These are historically disenfranchised populations, such as communities of color. The Foundation's listening campaign, by physically going to neighborhoods to hold these conversations increased the likelihood of reaching those often not asked for their input. Bell said, "The listening sessions were fundamental to the development of the strategy. We want to cycle back to the community. We held big sessions and smaller "consultative" sessions. We had a final session that led to the focus on people, place, and power."[24]

The Foundation has also relied on a network of faith leaders to help understand and connect to communities. Bell spoke of this effort, "Our FAITHS initiative is a network of faith leaders from around the nation that has been around for 25 years. This has helped us understand what has been happening in communities. They have been partnering us and helping us include people from all walks of life in our sessions."[25] The leadership of the foundation is a relevant variable as well. Fred Blackwell is from the region and predisposed to connecting in the community and pursuing their input. Duncan Robertson, the foundation's Board Chair said of Fred and his relationship to the community, "Gaining community voice is one of Fred's great attributes. Fred sees himself as part of the community. His whole life has been about understanding the community we most want to impact. Fred will continue to be in the role of convening conversations and listening. This is what Fred does."[26]

Building alliances is not only valuable in informing the development of strategic directions, but in helping to execute the desired agenda. In order to bring about greater regional equity, the San Francisco Foundation must look beyond themselves. Robertson declared, "We are bringing in partners – other nonprofits, corporate, City government – we can't do this alone. There is no way the San Francisco Foundation can do this alone."[27] For example, the foundation has been participating in a citywide partnership led by the City of San Francisco called, Hope SF. This effort has been bringing together City agencies, affordable housing developers, community-based organizations, foundations and others to rebuild public housing, enhance the lives of residents of public housing, and revitalize their neighborhoods.[28] For Dee Dee Brantley, not only is collaboration crucial to the foundation's success, its ability to initiate partnerships and bring different stakeholders together demonstrates its civic leadership. It is more than a grant making entity. Its commitment to regional equity is manifested in its institutional civic leadership. Brantley noted, "Our convening power will take us much further than the dollars we have. We can bring all of these different groups together to talk about issues and act as a neutral body to bring in the government, partners, other foundations, etc. Since some of the things we are trying to do are so complex, leveraging our voice to bring in more voices and more money. That is where our power is."[29]

Overall, the foundation has deepened its external engagement to gain greater input from neighborhoods in the region it serves. As Robertson said, "We force ourselves to continue to engage the community." He continued, "At the Trustee level and in management and staff, there is an anxiousness to ask, are we doing the right thing?"[30] As the foundation evolves under a new strategy, it is continuing to figure out how to institutionalize securing feedback from the community in a meaningful and actionable manner. The Foundation is considering how to embed listening campaigns into their ongoing work. Manifesting a commitment to equity and inclusion in external relations is one challenge. The Foundation is also making important transitions toward living up to a commitment to equity and inclusion internally.

How Inclusion Informs Strategy Institutionally

While the foundation has been committed to principles such as equity and inclusion for many years, the nature of how staff operate, how grants are made, and how programs are designed have been shifting. Robertson reflected on institutional changes from the last President to the current one. He said, "There were five different program areas with a program officer – they operated in silos. The Foundation was the broader umbrella for the five program areas. The programs did not connect with each other."[31] He continued, "There has been turnover of people, particularly at the executive level. There is a different tone at the top. There was a tagline, 'We invest in change.' But, internally, the foundation struggled with its own change. The new staff are more interested in working on a broader level – less focused. The Foundation used to attract people with a particular expertise. These staff are happy to collaborate across programs."[32] Bell said of these changes, "Programming has been reorganized. There are intersections that are addressed. Budgeting and decision-making have been impacted. The program department was structured as a collection of franchises with their own budgets and own approaches. There was little collaboration. There were a lot of one-year smaller grants. Now their average grants are $80k and many more are multi-year."[33]

This broader regional equity strategy that transcends traditional program boundaries calls for new thinking about intersections across the issue areas that many foundations tend to support – education, health, the arts, etc. As a veteran at the foundation, Dee Dee Brantley sees value in the new approach. She reflected, "The beauty of this is that you don't look at these things in isolation. You don't look at art as how to retain art in and of itself, but how does art get us to an equity focus? You cannot reach economic or racial equity without education; but you might look at education in the sense that how can certain things in education cause inequities. Therefore, it's all towards this greater goal. It is more of a focus around equity, causing the foundation to create population level change."[34]

Fred Blackwell wanted the foundation to aspire to a broader vision as well as a different approach that would transcend their prior mode of operating. This kind of change requires a shift in organizational culture and takes time to implement. Personnel changes can facilitate such an adaptation. But even new staff have to adjust to practices new to the institution, and new to philanthropy. The notion of semi-autonomous, distinct programs in a Foundation is far closer to the norm than a commitment to a broad vision such as regional equity. This programmatic transition ultimately affects grants. In this case, as the foundation's strategic planning process was underway, grantees were informed of the foundation's evolving priorities.

Renewed priorities informed by inclusion of community voices are reshaping how the foundation designs and implements its work. This means not only a new staff for the sake of having a new staff, but identifying a particular type of employee. This means new job descriptions that can adequately convey different desired qualities in candidates. Blackwell indicated, "We are more cognizant about who we hire. For example, the Program Officer job description is a little different. Internally, there's an expectation to be able to work across pathways in the Program department. There is less of an expectation that people are content experts in particular areas and more [being] able to synthesize... less about being a filter of proposals and more about being a leader of a body of work."[35]

The Foundation has shifted toward multi-year larger grants versus smaller grants over a single year. However, smaller grants are available. The Foundation instituted a "rapid response" fund for organizations with smaller budgets. These grants help small organizations "respond to issues in their communities in nimble ways."[36] Structurally, one of the challenges with strategic grantmaking is the tendency to leave out smaller organizations that either do not have budgets large enough for foundations to consider them from grants or do not fit perfectly within program strategies. These smaller grants provide balance in tandem with larger grants and accessibility to grassroots organizations.

Every aspect of the foundation's systems and operations are under consideration in attempting to reflect a renewed commitment to equity and inclusion. Brantley referenced the need for changes in technological systems to help measure impact. She said, "We are doing a huge technology transition right now to a new system called Flux. What we are realizing is that we need to collect a lot more data. With all of this you need to know whether or not people are better off. So, we are holding ourselves more accountable to measure more impact."[37] Another important factor is how the foundation contracts with vendors. "You need to make a conscious effort to diversify your vendor list and employees. It should not just be who you've worked with the last 20 years." Brantley added.[38]

This new strategy focused on regional equity also has implications for how the foundation interacts with donors. Ruben Orduna reflected on how changes at the foundation have impacted his work. He said, "What I am doing is not just fundraising but mobilizing resources. How to find resources that would never traditionally go to the foundation but can change its direction. My role is changing because we have the ability to influence the way donors are thinking about their philanthropy. We want donors to think more broadly and apply an equity lens to [their] thinking."[39] This is a compelling approach for a community foundation – engaging donors in a way that encourages a particular perspective or "lens". It appears the foundation has become a different place as an institution. Its policies and practices are increasingly reflecting a philosophical commitment to a set of values and a vision for regional equity.

Progress – What Has Been the Impact of these Approaches? How is Progress Measured?

As their plan for greater regional equity is in its early stages, it is difficult to assess impact on such a multidimensional concept. But there are a couple of levels of assessment worth pondering. First of all, the strategic direction in itself – the idea of a community foundation prioritizing regional equity with an emphasis on racial equity, and the process by which the foundation arrived at this conclusion. A few variables are relevant with respect to the content of the foundation's strategic direction, particularly regarding the concept of inclusion.

The Foundation took an intentionally inclusive approach to setting their agenda on a new course with an emphasis on community engagement. This began at the Board level prior to Blackwell's arrival. The Board made a conscious decision to identify a new President who would be predisposed to structuring techniques to communicate with constituents across the region and incorporate their input into shaping the foundation's future around pressing local needs. The Board wanted to transcend previous approaches taken by the foundation yet remain true to a historical commitment to equity and social justice. In hiring Fred Blackwell, the Board brought in an African American man born and raised in the region. Therefore, the foundation hired someone representative of constituents in the region with lived experiences cognizant of what it means to be a native of the region. This insight also brings an understanding of how the region has evolved over time.

Regional equity as a priority is a function of the region's evolution. The region's economy grew in a way that exacerbated inequities and altered the security of lower income residents and shifted the demographic balance in the area. Blackwell also represented local government, having been a public official in Oakland – a city which has experienced some of the most significant residential inflation, gentrification, and displacement. The regional equity strategic priority is also a reflection of the listening campaign, which was a deliberate pursuit of inclusion. The campaign intentionally convened community residents in neighborhoods across the region to discuss the issues they are facing and how the foundation can address them. Indeed, the residents experience inequality and recognize the significance of race in widening disparities in the region. The idea of emphasizing regional equity in the foundation's approach with attention to people, place, and power is a function of leadership from the Board and President as well as the wisdom of the communities comprising the region. If the foundation followed a different path, perhaps regional equity with strong consideration of racial equity would not be the foundation's plan. It is important to assess impact on this level – the content of the plan itself. The Foundation dedicated itself to regional equity, in large part, because of these factors.

This content is significant because it demonstrates that inclusion can help a foundation crystallize the real issues. The Foundation engaged constituents in society in order to better understand the real concerns facing the communities they serve. And this influenced the content of the resulting plan. Who is included in shaping planning makes a difference. The Foundation's version of strategic philanthropy broadened its based of stakeholders, which resulted in, not a narrowing of program priorities, but a broader point of view. The Foundation is now grappling with how to transcend traditional philanthropic program divisions and make truly multi-issue investments. This will likely be a continuous challenge. But in recognizing the lived experiences of constituents in the community, the foundation is working hard to develop systems and structures reflecting a commitment to achieving regional equity.

These systems and structures represent another level on which the foundation's progress to date can be assessed. How has the foundation's grantmaking changed? How is the foundation operating differently to position the institution towards becoming a greater catalyst for regional equity? On the level of grantmaking, the foundation rearranged its guidelines to reflect a commitment to regional equity, and organized submissions within the categories of People, Place, and Power. Existing grantees and organizations that were not already receiving funds applied through an open cycle. Note that existing grantees, during the strategic planning process, received "transition grants" prior to the open cycle. Fred Blackwell, provided some data that resulted from their process. He said, "A few numbers: 40% of folks we funded through the open cycle came back. Almost half of the grants were multiyear. Before all were 12 month-long. Average grant size was $80,000. Used to be $20,000–$22,000. 70% of grants were made to organizations that are led by people of color."[40]

In order to bring about greater regional equity, the foundation thought it would be important to provide multi-year grants at larger amounts. Given the long-range nature of achieving regional equity, it made sense to them to treat the magnitude of the challenge appropriately and provide grantees longer time horizons. The process did not eliminate existing grantees, as the data demonstrates, but the process yielded many new grantees. There were organizations engaging in work consistent with the foundation's priorities in the neighborhood throughout the region that were not receiving investments from the foundation before. And it is also clear that many of the organizations working in the communities where the foundation has found the greatest need are led by people of color.

The Foundation also made some substantive programmatic shifts, adding work on criminal justice and moving away from a focus on health given that many other foundations in the region are funding health. Judith Bell said of the process, "We received 960 applications and funded 144 in our first cycle. We are opening our doors with the open grants cycle. We want to be transparent about what we are seeking. This is a balancing act because we are a community foundation – we want to be accountable to the community."[41] The grantmaking process in itself has been an act of inclusion. In strategic philanthropy, foundations often carefully select grantees, sometimes already well-known to the institution. An open cycle process is often associated with a less targeted approach. But the San Francisco Foundation combined the ideas of presenting strategic priorities and goals within a broad framework with an open call for proposals from organizations in the region working toward some dimension of regional equity affecting people, place, and power in the Bay Area. Obviously, such an open process yielded a substantial number of proposals. But it did help the foundation find many new organizations, along with existing grantees.

Beyond the open cycle, the foundation is taking unprecedented steps toward regional equity. As housing is a central concern with regard to inequities in the region, the foundation is investing in housing bonds. Bell said of this endeavor, "The region is in a tremendous housing crisis. We have supported substantial housing bonds in the region. We are paying attention to protection, preservation, and production. In this strategy, we moved c4 and c3 resources. As a community foundation, we can move c4 resources. They only have $1 million to do this (investing in c4s), but we used it, and it was successful. We set the stage for a powerful statement."[42] This is an area where the foundation has positioned itself to take less traditional paths to underscore the urgency of housing affordability. Investing in bonds and 501c4 organizations that are able to advocate around policy changes are two ways in which the foundation has added to its repertoire of ways to address regional equity.

As the overall regional equity strategy evolves, assessing the impact of its grants and investments will become an even greater priority. Blackwell said of this reality, "A big push for me this year, is data. We are now on a third stage: first was being clear about what we meant, second was rolling out implementation, and third is evaluating impact. In real time, that is where the foundation is at."[43] These three stages reflect the evolution of the planning process. They can demonstrate impact, particularly in relation to inclusion, at each stage. In being clear about what they meant, the foundation leveraged community voices to shape this clarity. In rolling out implementation, the foundation widely disseminated its intentions, opened up its process, and brought in numerous new

and existing grantees with multi-year grants. The foundation is currently designing and constructing the third stage.

Blackwell continued with respect to evaluation, "In the Bay Area, the foundation is not known for evaluation and discipline around data. It is not what we
are known for; but [we] are working hard to change that. Last year's budget
included a new position – Director for Strategic Learning and Evaluation, and we
brought on a second person in the program department."[44] The Foundation is
also beginning to partner with the Annie E. Casey Foundation, a national foundation based in Baltimore, Maryland, to bring in a concept called results-based
leadership. This concept is designed to build the capacity of leaders to focus their
efforts on results. It is based on the *results-based accountability*, which stresses
defining results and holding people and groups accountable by using data to
demonstrate progress.[45]

Blackwell indicated that they are "developing targets for each pathway and
converting to [a] new business intelligence system that will allow them to be
more diligent about extracting data." For Blackwell, this is not simply a matter of
collecting data for its sake. He said, "sharing what we are learning is an important
part of civic leadership."[46] This thinking is interesting in itself, as it speaks to
communication with constituents. The Foundation included a broader constituency in shaping the commitment to regional equity. The expectation is to be
able to demonstrate progress toward that commitment. As previously noted, the
breadth of the undertaking of regional equity in the areas of people, place, and
power is tremendous and far beyond what the foundation can do alone. Data and
the evaluation processes leading to data would have to take into account these
complexities. It appears the foundation is very cognizant of these dynamics. It will
be interesting to see how evaluation mechanisms will reflect the range of tools,
practices, and partnerships the foundation will employ on its journey.

Conclusions and Lessons Learned (Including Implications for the Particular Type of Foundation)

The San Francisco Foundation is a case of a philanthropic institution with a historical commitment to its region and to values of social justice; these values
recently entered a new era with significant departures from the way the foundation operates. The Foundation employed new techniques in order to reach a
broader cross section of its constituency, such as a listening campaign and an open
grants cycle. These practices reinforced the foundation's longstanding values and
principles but provided greater programmatic and structural specificity regarding a
commitment to regional equity with an emphasis on racial equity. While a strategy highlighting regional equity is completed, the San Francisco Foundation story
remains one of transition.

Looking forward, there are lessons to reflect upon and areas for growth in the
future. Evaluation and impact have already been noted as a significant evolving

priority. A greater emphasis on race is another consideration. Blackwell sees an "opening to talk about race and income and wealth disparities as a result of the current political climate. The climate is one that is challenging and frustrating but is also encouraging in that it has sparked an openness and willingness to talk about thorny issues. If we can harness it in the right way, then it has some potential."[47] He is encouraged by the opportunity, but also concerned about the persistence and exacerbation of racial inequities in California. California is often viewed as an accepting and progressive society. Blackwell wondered, "In the current political climate, a lot of folks are looking to California as a leader. On the one hand, there are a lot of positives about the state. But the fact that California's perception of itself is out of line with reality with regards to race is concerning."[48] This will be a substantial challenge ahead for the foundation as it continues to interface across demographics, industries, and socioeconomic levels. Effective communication about race will be crucial to furthering dialogues and action around racial equity.[49]

Duncan Robertson also looks forward to deepening the foundation's commitment to equity. He feels a sense of urgency about equity in the region. He speculated, "I am excited about addressing the disparities in equity. I worry that, if we don't do something, the Bay Area will not be the same in 25 years."[50] Institutional change will remain a consideration for the future. As the staff are embarking on a new way of operating to reflect the foundation's commitment to regional equity in practice, the foundation has been holding monthly internal sessions designed to help staff understand and act on equity. But the pathway to changing any institution's culture is lengthy. Judith Bell recognizes the importance of this direction. She reflected and looked ahead, "There are people who have worked in the foundation for over 30 years. We underestimated the need for change management. Change management will continue to be required. This is about changing the culture of the foundation. It is hard to change culture, and it is hard for people to trust that change is underway."[51] This reality demonstrates how much of a change in culture it can be for a foundation to commit to a broad agenda such as regional equity, transcending traditional program boundaries and remaining accountable to numerous external constituents. Indeed, all foundations are unique in their own way because there are so many historical and contextual factors that inform a foundation's priorities and practices. However, the San Francisco Foundation is grappling with changing behavior that is closer to the norm in foundations (i.e. programs operating in silos).

Bell continued, "We are reinventing ourselves; and we have to continue our partnership with communities – we are going back to listen to communities. We are going to build on our partnership with donors, which will increase our capacity for change. Most of what we give away comes from donors."[52] The Foundation intends to deepen its engagement with local communities. This bridge to ongoing engagement with external constituents is becoming institutionalized in the foundation. It is becoming a method to shape how the foundation contributes to regional equity and remains accountable to its region. Bell also speaks to another important feature in a community foundation's reality – connecting with donors. A community foundation must be a partner with both the constituents who execute and are affected by efforts to improve their target region and donors. Sometimes these constituents overlap. For example, many community foundations are actively seeking to diversify the demographics of their donor bases and creating ways for people at varying income levels to contribute (i.e. giving circles).

Ruben Orduna notices the increase in giving to an equity agenda. So, to some degree, donors are buying into the foundation's direction. But donors are multidimensional. One challenge for the future will be to persuade a broader and broader cross section of donors that regional equity is a major priority. He said, "There's a lot of bandwidth with the donors. They're not all one note. You have to remember that a foundation has many interests. Our donors are that way too. We have to inspire them and make them better-informed citizens of the region, then you're going to be a better person and see the inequities around you."[53]

Brantley, having been at the foundation for seventeen years, is hopeful about the foundation's ability to bring about regional equity. She thinks that they have been very cognizant of what it will take to influence such substantial change in the region. When asked if she is confident about the foundation's ability to bring about regional equity, she replied, "I am. I believe that it is possible. If I didn't I shouldn't be here. Part of the reason is I believe we are realistic. We can't do it alone. I think this is a good approach. Some of the evidence of that is that we are getting new partners who want to work with us. We don't have a specific number but I do believe we are going to make an impact."[54]

Indeed, the foundation is positioning itself to be judged based on its ability to facilitate regional equity. It appears this is the foundation's desire at this point. They want to be clear and public about their commitment to a comprehensive agenda that was informed by the public. They want to establish systems to track their progress around regional equity, but they are aware that their role is not only a grantmaker, but a civic leader that catalyzes others into action around this agenda. They desire additional partnerships with organizations across industries. They recognize that engagement with the private sector could be among their most significant challenges ahead.

The foundation is a community foundation. It is one of the larger such entities in existence. It has a rich tradition. It is not dispensing with the community foundation model despite its numerous structural and cultural institutional changes. But it is defining the community foundation model for itself – it is expanding what it means to engage its community. All community foundations are a reflection of their regions, but the San Francisco Foundation is deliberately organizing its programmatic direction around the community's articulated needs. It is willing to change its modes of operating. It is not bound by tradition, yet it respects the foundation's history. It is in the process of defining a new way of doing business for community foundations.

Notes

1 (San Francisco Foundation, *About – History*, 2019)
2 (San Francisco Foundation, *The Numbers*, 2019)
3 (San Francisco Foundation, *About – Mission Equity Values*, 2019)
4 ibid
5 (Foundation Center, Foundation Stats, 2019)
6 (Mazany and Perry 2013)
7 (CFLeads, *Homepage*, 2019)
8 (San Francisco Foundation, *Programs*, 2019)
9 (Interview, Blackwell 2018)
10 Ibid.
11 (Interview, Robertson 2018)
12 (Interview, Bell 2018)
13 (Interview, Brantley 2018)
14 (Interview, Blackwell 2018)
15 Ibid.
16 Ibid.
17 Ibid.
18 (Interview, Orduna 2018)
19 (National Philanthropic Trust 2018)
20 (Interview, Bell 2018)
21 (Interview, Blackwell 2018)
22 Ibid.
23 (Interview, Bell 2018)
24 Ibid.
25 Ibid.
26 (Interview, Robertson 2018)
27 Ibid.
28 (HOPE SF, *Partners – Overview*, 2013)
29 (Interview, Brantley 2018)
30 (Interview, Robertson 2018)
31 Ibid.
32 Ibid.
33 (Interview, Bell 2018)
34 (Interview, Brantley 2018)
35 (Interview, Blackwell 2018)
36 Ibid.
37 (Interview, Brantley 2018)
38 Ibid.
39 (Interview, Orduna 2018)
40 (Interview, Blackwell 2018)
41 (Interview, Bell 2018)
42 Ibid.
43 (Interview, Blackwell 2018)
44 Ibid.
45 (The Annie E. Casey Foundation, 2013)
46 (Interview, Blackwell 2018)
47 (Interview, Blackwell 2018)
48 Ibid.
49 The San Francisco Foundation has been participating in a learning exchange among foundations called the Race and Equity in Philanthropy Group (REPG). REPG selects different themes to address in these discussions. Communications about race is the

latest topic being addressed by foundations in this group. Upon the completion of a series of exchanges on this topic, case studies of participating foundations' experiences in communications about race will be prepared and included in a report for public consumption.

50 (Interview, Robertson 2018)
51 (Interview, Bell 2018)
52 Ibid.
53 (Interview, Orduna 2018)
54 (Interview, Brantley 2018)

References

Bell, Judith. Interview with David Maurrasse. Telephone Interview. New York, March 7, 2018.

Blackwell, Fred. Interview with David Maurrasse. Personal Interview. San Francisco, February 7, 2018.

Brantley, Dee Dee. Interview with David Maurrasse. Personal Interview. San Francisco, February 7, 2018.

CFLeads, *Homepage*, 2019. http://www.cfleads.org/ (accessed March 20, 2019).

Foundation Center. *Foundation Stats*. 2019. http://data.foundationcenter.org/#/foundations/ (accessed March 25, 2019).

HOPE SF. *Partners – Overview*. 2013. http://hope-sf.org/partner.php#partners (accessed March 20, 2019).

Mazany, Terry, and David C. Perry, eds. *Here for Good: Community Foundations and the Challenges of the 21st Century*. ME Sharpe, 2013.

National Philanthropic Trust. *The 2018 DAF Report*. 2018. https://www.nptrust.org/daf-report/sponsor-type-comparison.html#community-foundations (accessed March 20, 2019).

Orduna, Ruben. Interview with David Maurrasse. Personal Interview. San Francisco, February 7, 2018.

Robertson, Duncan. Interview with David Maurrasse. Telephone Interview. New York, February 8, 2018.

San Francisco Foundation. *About – History*. 2019. https://sff.org/about-tsff/about-our-work/history-of-tsff/ (accessed March 20, 2019).

San Francisco Foundation. *About – Mission Equity Values*. 2019. https://sff.org/about-tsff/about-our-work/mission-equity-values/ (accessed March 20, 2019).

San Francisco Foundation. *Programs*. 2019. http://sff.org/programs/ (accessed March 20, 2019).

San Francisco Foundation. *The Numbers*. 2019. http://letskeepbuilding.sff.org/the-numbers/ (accessed March 20, 2019).

The Annie E. Casey Foundation. *Leading For Results – Developing Talent to Drive Change*. 2013. http://www.aecf.org/m/resourcedoc/aecf-LeadingforResults-2013.pdf#page=4 (accessed March 23, 2019).

5

GLOBAL PHILANTHROPY
Conrad Hilton Foundation

Background on the Conrad Hilton Foundation

In 1919, Conrad Hilton founded a globally recognizable brand. He bought his first hotel in Cisco, Texas during the oil boom of the time. In 1944, he established the Conrad N. Hilton Foundation (hereinafter called the Hilton Foundation) as a philanthropic trust. The foundation was established as a nonprofit corporation that was a separate entity from Hilton Hotels in 1950. When Conrad Hilton died in 1979 at 91 years of age, he left over 99% of his multi-million dollar estate as a donation to the foundation.[1] In his will, he mandates that the foundation should focus on specific problem areas:

1. relieve the suffering, the distressed, and the destitute;
2. shelter little children with the umbrella of your charity;
3. support the Catholic Sisters, who devote their love and life's work for the good of mankind; and
4. let there be no territorial, religious, or other color restrictions on your benefactions. The last will leaves latitude for the board of directors to translate noble goals into specific, practical actions.[2]

Today, the foundation is still guided by the will of its founder as many of its strategies and programs reflect Conrad Hilton's wishes for the future. Additionally, it has become one of the larger philanthropic foundations in the world with an asset base of over US$2.5 billion, which consistently sees net returns on its investments year-over-year.

The foundation's assets experienced a dramatic spike in 2009 mainly due to the foundation's unrealized gains and transfer of net assets upon acquiring the

Conrad N. Hilton Fund, a private foundation effectively controlled by the same persons.[3]

In the future, the foundation will likely experience another substantial infusion of additional capital. Barron Hilton, the son of Conrad Hilton, who joined the foundation in 1950, pledged to leave 97% of his $2.3 billion estates to the foundation upon his death.[4] Staff members expect that this contribution will both double the asset base and number of employees after Barron Hilton passes away. He was born in October 1927 and his estate is now worth almost $4.5 billion.[5]

By 2016, the Conrad N. Hilton Foundation's total assets reached over $2,692 million, with long-term investments of over $2,598 million.[6] Its annual total grantmaking had steadily increased to about $112 million by 2018, covering various areas such as Catholic sisters, foster youth, homelessness, substance use prevention, young children affected by HIV and AIDS, disaster relief and recovery, hospitality workforce development, and others.[7] Since its inception, the foundation has made 547 domestic grants in the U.S. and 282 international grants, all of which totaled about $1.8 billion with roughly $112.5 million of both domestic and international grants made in 2017.[8]

International Strategy and Sustainable Development Goals Commitment

This chapter focuses particularly on the international dimension of the Hilton Foundation's giving strategy. Engaging grantee and grantee constituent communities, for a U.S.-based foundation takes on a particular dynamics internationally, especially in developing countries in the global south. Global giving among a few U.S.-based foundations is an important aspect of the fabric of the philanthropic

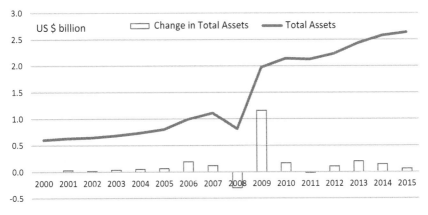

FIGURE 5.1 Total Assets and the Yearly Change for the Hilton Foundation since 2000
Note: total assets measured at the end of year using book value
Source: ProPublica 2019b

field. It requires particular considerations and competencies distinct from domestic giving. Each country represents a unique context, in many cases, dramatically different from that of the United States. Any foundations seeking to be successful in these contexts must consider numerous factors.

Despite the few similarities between domestic and global grantmaking, giving outside the United States can be challenging and rewarding for domestic foundations. Lengthy physical distances, cultural barriers, language differences and different legal systems are only some of the explicit factors that contribute to the complexity and difficulty of international grantmaking. However, according to the report, *The State of Global Giving by US Foundations: 2011–2015*, [9] international giving by U.S. foundations reached an unprecedented high level of $9.3 billion in 2015, with a growth rate of 306% from $2.1 billion in 2002. In terms of the grantmaking channels, only 12% of the dollars granted by U.S. foundations went to locally based organizations in the grant-receiving countries; the rest were channeled via organizations based elsewhere.

One important consideration in international giving is how external foundations interact with local populations. If these financial investments designed to improve certain conditions elsewhere are not guided by the wisdom and lived experiences of local populations, can they be effective? How to fund *with* rather than *for* local constituents has confronted international giving for many decades. The Hilton Foundation has been grappling with these dynamics.

The Hilton Foundation has been a pioneer and notable actor in global giving. Its endeavors in international grantmaking are well known. Edmund J. Cain, who was the Vice President of Grant Programs overseeing all domestic and international grant programming (including overall responsibility for the foundation's strategic planning) retired in December 2018.[10] He argues that philanthropy tends to parachute itself in with the best of intentions and pick issues and areas and then find an industrious NGO and move forward. "They are not contributing to systematic solutions," argues Cain, "and it is important to work with local actors before starting grantmaking."[11] Cain added, "Philanthropies have found that it is important to be associated with the Sustainable Development Goals (SDGs[12]). All of the countries where we are working fully embrace the SDGs and aspirational frameworks. But some philanthropies did not even know these goals existed. We are trying to sensitize the sector around the fact that they need to understand the environment in which they are working."

Cain reflected on when he sat in a meeting held by a committee of the Council on Foundations[13] (COF) on the topic of international philanthropy. He asked the meeting participants (which included foundations such as the Bill and Melinda Gates Foundation, the Ford Foundation, and others) whether COF was focused on the SDGs. Some indicated their unwillingness to work within existing frameworks. Cain suggested foundations have to be educated about what it takes to facilitate significant change. Outside of the U.S., the SDGs are being taken very seriously as aspirational goals. "There is an overinflated image in philanthropy and humility drives our values at the Hilton Foundation," says Cain. He continued, "One can only move the needle with all hands on deck, and philanthropy can play an important role."[14]

Cain refers to the importance of the mindset that foundations bring to their giving and interaction with intended beneficiary populations. He emphasizes humility as an essential characteristic to bring to philanthropic strategy. Each individual foundation can contribute only so much to a particular social or economic concern. Cain sees a broader framework such as the SDGs as an established effort galvanizing numerous partners across sectors around a commitment to demonstrable improvements in a number of priority areas that overlap with the strategic priorities of numerous foundations. Philanthropy tends to struggle with the combination of pursuing clear goals and integrating constituent perspectives into those intentions. Simultaneously being responsive yet strategic can elude many foundations. The challenge of incorporating philanthropic strategy into existing frameworks is another important aspect of Cain's commentary. Each foundation has a mission, purpose, and strategy. But there is no guarantee that each foundation's priorities are aligned with existing agendas designed to address similar concerns. Cain indicates that a certain degree of institutional humility is required for a foundation to integrate its strategy into another plan determined elsewhere.

Like most philanthropic institutions, the Hilton Foundation has evolved throughout its history. The thinking illustrated by Cain was not always the foundation's approach. According to Cain, the first era of the foundation under Conrad Hilton was characterized by serendipitous grantmaking.[15] Then there was a period under Donald H. Hubbs. He was the Chairman and Chief Executive Officer from 1998 to 2005, when the foundation emphasized project grantmaking, and gave a few organizations major grants. Cain arrived in 2006. This was a period in which strategic philanthropy was on the rise (Mark Kramer,[16] etc.). Cain communicated with Mark Kramer about where the Hilton Foundation stood at the time in relation to strategic grantmaking. They have identified areas that are neglected, and then established infrastructure, in which newly hired staff are assigned to monitoring, evaluation and learning. Each strategic area has a partner assessing the foundation's impact. A document describes their strategy – capturing their overarching vision.[17] It speaks to three pillars – programmatic, systemic change, and then learning.

Strategic philanthropy stresses focused giving leading toward greater impact. However, it does not guarantee who participates in shaping strategic directions. Getting to the intended beneficiary populations in international giving requires deliberate planning. When interfacing with organizations in other countries, the foundation's approaches have been continuously changing. At an earlier stage, the foundation was very dependent on international NGOs and grant makers. Some options in international grantmaking include: i) request a local partner bring in multiple stakeholders to inform the foundation's strategy in that sector and what a foundation can do to affect those issues; ii) work with international NGOs that are most aligned with the foundation's strategy, and depend on them to make sure the foundation's strategies are realized; iii) build capacity of local government.

Another way is to use the SDG Philanthropy Platform[18] in some of the countries in which a foundation works. The SDG Philanthropy Platform incorporates national governments into philanthropic conversations. Since the UNDP has a natural convening role with governments and with the SDGs, countries are taking much of the weight of implementation. In this regard, philanthropy can help national governments' work toward SDGs. However, getting to populations with the lived experiences of the types of issues addressed in the SDGs (poverty, health, education…) is still another concern.

The Hilton Foundation works with local people who are familiar with local socioeconomic situations. In their work in Kenya, a local person is the foundation's eyes and ears on the ground. When the foundation does not have a local staff person in place, it typically works through other organizations based in those countries. In some instances, the foundation funds these local organizations. This approach deviates from how some other U.S.-based foundations are funding globally. The Ford Foundation and the Rockefeller Foundation, for example, tend to establish physical offices in the grant-receiving countries. However, a physical office would not necessarily preclude a foundation from engaging with local constituents. The Hilton Foundation's approach may bring its own set of benefits. But the Hilton Foundation would rather place programming locally in the hands of local organizations rather than setting up an office in Africa. Specifically, almost all of the Hilton Foundation's grant-making process is conducted jointly with local partners in 17 countries in Africa (particularly in sub-Saharan Africa) in order to leverage the SDG Philanthropy Platform and the local philanthropic resources. The foundation's philanthropic practices and impact in Africa is discussed further in this chapter.

As the Director of Strategic Partnerships, Shaheen Kassim-Lakha points out, "We are not an operating foundation, and the foundation has to look for partners who really understand how to build capacity and work with local governments."[19] For example, to accelerate the coverage of reliable access to safe and affordable water services, the foundation partnered with IRC (the WHO International Reference Center on Community Water Supply[20]), which is based in the Netherlands, to focus on creating government capacity and improving international and local access for delivery.

Monitoring, Evaluation and Learning (MEL)[21] partners also help the foundation understand the local context and relevant ways to address issues in those contexts as a constant feedback loop. As Kassim-Lakha indicates, "We have local partners and are very dependent on staff traveling to hold annual convenings and do site visits; and the SDG Philanthropy Platform is a great way to do similar work without creating an office."[22] In the foundation's collaboration with other entities, the foundation also funds some NGOs directly to do the work as well as entities which regrant to other organizations. These are two distinct approaches when considering local engagement – effectively outsourcing to other organizations that represent and are familiar with the local context, and selecting local organizations to act as grantmaking entities by regranting to other local organizations. These are all structural and philosophical considerations that demonstrate the range of ways in which a foundation can choose how to best establish local lines of communication. Whichever framework is employed, the challenge is to ensure communication flows with local populations that shape foundation priorities. Additionally, in order to have a greater impact, foundations with shared interests in particular regions could combine their resources.

The Hilton Foundation has pursued collaboration with other philanthropists to develop an efficient framework for international philanthropy. Cain recalled his collaboration with Heather Grady, who is now a Vice President in Rockefeller Philanthropy Advisors' San Francisco office and leads the organization's strategy and program development in global philanthropy. At the time, she was based at the Rockefeller Foundation. With Brad Smith, the President and CEO of the Foundation Center, Cain and Grady looked to create an infrastructure to guide philanthropy in nations such as Ghana, Colombia, Indonesia, Zambia and others. In this endeavor, they were hoping that the various national governments could see value in structured collaboration with philanthropy. Kenya is where this approach has had a tremendous impact, according to Cain.

Through the "SDG Partnership Platform", Cain and other global philanthropy practitioners hear from community leaders and the private sector as an entry point. Cain indicated, "Although very few are willing to fund this kind of approach, the foundation has been in Ghana for 30 years. The SDGs help establish a systemic change framework designed to improve local residents' ability to get universal access to safe water and transportation. The Hilton Foundation's involvement has helped create a framework. The resources are finite and the issues are so daunting. These highly participatory processes led to frameworks like SDGs."[23]

The Hilton Foundation wants to be the catalyst to move forward to the framework they have been developing internationally. Cain hopes different actors will see the value of these collaborative frameworks (similar to those they established in Ghana and Kenya). The foundation wants to play an advocacy role around the importance of this kind of collaborative design. Here again, a couple of dimensions are apparent in how the Hilton Foundation conceptualizes and implements local engagement. One important feature is how the foundation is willing to work within an existing framework, via national governments' SDG commitments. Another is how the foundation collaborates to solicit feedback from local constituents to help inform the work going forward.

Cain also reflected on the problems and challenges confronting the foundation's international strategy and commitment. He recalled some resistance to the development of collaborative frameworks, particularly in philanthropy more generally. Cain maintains "It was a no brainer that philanthropy should support these collaborative networks, although foundations tend to be project-oriented."[24] The Global Humanitarian Conference in Istanbul a few years ago revealed a study that less than 1% of funds reach the communities. Therefore, Cain argues "We have to identify how to get to where the resources are really needed and there is a fiduciary responsibility. A part of the issue is channeling money to 501c3 organizations. The money has to get to the most effective and efficient service providers. Another challenge is that the private sector might now leap over philanthropy around these frameworks. Localization was another challenge for philanthropies and there are a few foundations looking at how to be more rooted."[25]

It is clear that the Hilton Foundation has been reflecting on appropriate techniques in order to ensure that grants are actually reaching intended beneficiary communities. The foundation is aware of the ways in which participatory methods can be counter to established philanthropic culture. Therefore, Cain and colleagues have been playing an active role in engaging other foundations about how to rework their approaches to international grantmaking. Cain referred to the "project" orientation of much of philanthropy. This tendency stresses narrow, highly focused, approaches to grantmaking that are designed to be easily measured. Shorter term projects with very defined prospective outcomes are not necessarily consistent with how constituents with lived experiences think. Open dialogue with constituents about their circumstances may raise issues that don't necessarily fit neatly within boundaries. Cain also identified the structural challenge of incorporated nonprofit organizations. Particularly in developing countries, but in low income communities in the developed countries as well, incorporated organizations are not necessarily the best change agents or most representative of constituent populations.

Strategic Commitment to Equity and Inclusion and Operational Structures

While foundation strategies to engage externally are crucial to demonstrating a commitment to values that recognize the significance of enabling local wisdom to drive philanthropic strategy, equity and inclusion can be reflected in a foundation's policies and systems as well. In international grantmaking, a demonstration of equity and inclusion in institutional practice can take on particular dimensions. As already indicated, the Hilton Foundation has systematized how it engages in local communities in the countries in which it invests. But the composition of the foundation's staff and Board as a whole, how the foundation spends beyond grant dollars, how the foundation communicates its priorities, how the foundation measures the demographics of grantees, how the foundation establishes policies on grantmaking, and various other areas comprise an institutional commitment. A foundation that is comprehensively dedicated to values such as equity and inclusion examines every facet of its institution and its practices.

Most foundations maintain a social purpose embedded in their mission statements. The statement Hilton's founder left was to "relieve the suffering, the distressed, and the destitute." "Today, the foundation invests in nonprofits working to alleviate human suffering around the world without regard to race, religion, or country."[26] Therefore, although diversity, equity, and inclusion (DEI) is a new term, the idea has been instilled in the 11 program areas from the foundation's inception. Most grantees have received funding from the foundation for several consecutive years. Therefore, the value of long-term grants is not new for the foundation.

Various aspects of equity and inclusion for the foundation have been evolving since its formation and along with its development. First of all, despite its many years in existence, the Hilton Foundation remains a family foundation. The majority of its Board members are Hilton family members. This reality immediately impacts the demographic composition of the Board. The foundation was once led by corporate white men in 1944 without including women or people of color on the Board or staff. The foundation has been gradually diversifying its staff as one of its philanthropic approaches is defined as, "We are committed to diversity, equity, and inclusion as core principles interwoven throughout the fabric of the foundation and as a lens that guides us both internally and in how we do our work."[27] Six members of the Board of Directors are family members; five are not family members. The foundation has three women on the Board.[28] On staff, the foundation's Director of Talent and Culture is African American.

In international grantmaking, the background of decision-makers is a significant factor in shaping the nature and effectiveness of the work to be done. Regarding the foundation's commitment to equity and inclusion in international grantmaking, as Cain says, "one problem as an international grantmaker is whom you have on board."[29] For instance, Shaheen Kassim-Lakha is the Director of Strategic Partnerships and she had been the Director of International Programs from 2008 until June 2019.[30] Shaheen is a Kenyan who "has a broad academic and professional background in health services and public health, including experience in hospital administration, developing environmental health policy for urban centers in North America, and program management in several countries in Asia and Africa."[31] Shaheen Kassim-Lakha reflected on shifts in staffing, "The foundation's strategy changed to be more outcome-oriented and it moved away from a staff that had solid generalist skills to a staff that has specific international experience."[32]

Employees with local living and working experiences bring an understanding of local contexts and contribute to the effectiveness of the foundation's international programming. On the Board, the foundation's President, Peter Laugharn brings extensive international experience. He has 25 years of foundation and nonprofit experience internationally, particularly regarding improving the well-being of vulnerable children.[33] His international working experience includes six years serving as Executive Director of the Netherlands-based Bernard van Leer Foundation, and 11 years working in a variety of roles at Save the Children, while eight out of the 11 years he was based in Bamako, Mali. Cain commented, "When I got into the sector, I found it intriguing that there are so many foundations that have CEOs without international experience, yet so much international grantmaking."[34]

Institutionalization and Manifestations of International Development Commitment

Emily Skehan manages a portfolio of grants as part of the Special Programs team and oversees Hilton Foundation's family giving programs; and Jennifer Ho advises and supports the foundation's systems and processes that enable organizational learning, reflection and strategy improvement. They both elaborated on how a commitment to equity and inclusion is being systemically embedded into the institution. The Hilton Foundation has also been improving its inclusion and equity strategically in its grantmaking practices.

The Hilton Foundation has incorporated DEI into almost all aspects of its strategic operations both literally and practically. While it is not on the website and the Board doesn't definitively discuss it, DEI work is conducted all the time. Ho says, "Using DEI as a phrase has come up from various consultants, but the process of embracing it as a phrase is still ongoing. For a lot of the systemic work that the foundation does, the idea of inclusivity is at the forefront of strategic approaches. It is likely that the foundation's strategic redesign will include DEI language and a DEI plan."[35] As the Learning Officer, she is excited to propel the work of the MEL partners and implement a structure that increases impact.

Ho speaks to the realities of many foundations, particularly longstanding family foundations. Board members can represent a wide range of viewpoints. They may agree on the need for a foundation to be of assistance to particular vulnerable populations. But they might disagree on how to engage with and invest in those communities. Language plays an important role in how to find common ground across widely different political and social perspectives. How to frame the work from staff to the Board is crucial in many foundations, particularly larger institutions with numerous staff members. Some larger foundations that have been in existence for generations (i.e. the Ford Foundation or the Rockefeller Foundation or the W.K. Kellogg Foundation) may have very few family members on their Boards at this stage in their organizational life cycle. In some ways, the Hilton Foundation stands out in this regard. It was founded several decades ago, but it is still definitively a family foundation. Needless to say, foundation Boards are the ultimate decision makers in philanthropic institutions. Therefore, how staff communicate program priorities to Board members is essential to a foundation's functionality. The staff of Hilton are taking a particular approach to making sure that the foundation's work is framed in a way that resonates across the organization at all levels.

Additionally, the Hilton Foundation has been intentionally incorporating the perspectives of grantees and grantees' constituent populations in informing the foundation's decisions. Specifically, each of the Hilton Foundation's program areas holds annual convenings where grantees and constituents attend. Skehan said, "The foundation is not a facilitator of these events and instead makes them a place for partners and local actors to speak with each other about progress. At this point, the foundation is also working on institutionalizing DEI." As Skehan believes, the foundation falls on the higher end of the DEI spectrum because the Hilton Foundation usually has long-term grantee partnerships for marginalized people and has institutionalized mechanisms for incorporating their voices into decision-making.[36]

Skehan provided a day-to-day perspective of the foundation's work from her relevant five years' working experience at the foundation. She reflected, "There is no disconnect between DEI strategies and the Board of Directors because the DEI framework has not been definitively expressed to them yet."[37] She acknowledges that the language in the foundation's guiding mission statement might not be the most current; but their constituents, through their experiences with the foundation, would recognize the foundation's commitment to DEI. "For example, with disaster relief work, we are focused more on long-term sustainable recovery, instead of only providing emergency aid. In other words, we need to make sure that local actors are not only doing clean up but rebuilding in a sustainable way that sets their communities up for future potential resilience from similar events,"[38] Skehan stated. Incorporating the voices of those with lived experiences is a priority for the foundation, according to Skehan. Since they are the experts on the ground in their communities, having them express sustainable solutions to problems is valuable to the actual work. Skehan placed the idea of DEI in philanthropy into perspective, "Philanthropy itself exists because of inequities so we are here to fill gaps and need to have honest conversations about how to do that."[39] Skehan speaks to one of the great ironies in philanthropy – the wealth created in order to develop philanthropy as we know it, established and exacerbated economic inequities in society. She sees an inherent responsibility of philanthropy to communities that have been less economically advantaged as necessary to address historical imbalances.

In addition to monitoring and evaluating the effectiveness of the programs, the foundation brings in consultants to rework their funding areas to creating an internal "Diversity, Equity, and Inclusion Advisory Board" (led by the VP of Talent and Culture). This body is helping to develop a DEI plan for the foundation, particularly in anticipation of future growth and programmatic expansion. They are exploring how to diversify recruiting and conduct in-house professional development. With an expected doubling in the size of the foundation's staff, they hope to recruit a diverse array of professionals, who are also trained internally on DEI principles. The foundation also intends to conduct a full internal DEI audit in the future.

They are demonstrating an awareness of the connection between their external engagement with grantee and constituent populations and internal policies and practices. It is also interesting to observe the foundation's degree of foresight regarding their ultimate expansion, and the importance of instilling a commitment to DEI values as new staff are recruited and oriented.

Ho is a new employee (in her position for six months at the time of the interview) in a recently created position that acts as an internal advisor to oversee the strategic direction and the Monitoring, Evaluation and Learning (MEL).[40] In this capacity as a member of the foundation's "Kitchen Cabinet", Ho helps gather learning from programs. She sees DEI as very present in the minds of the foundation's program officers. The foundation is undergoing a systemic shift keeping in mind how to organize programming in a manner that is most beneficial to grantees and their communities. "The foundation is on a journey away from the traditional grantmaking approach of charitable giving", says Ho, "...it is much more focused on capacity building today than in the past."[41] But with the reality of the Board's perspective on how DEI is situated in their messaging, it is simultaneously very apparent that the staff is leading substantive changes internally that will affect programming as well as systems and operations.

Both Skeehan and Ho hope to see a more explicit institutional DEI strategy in place in the next couple of years. At this stage, the foundation continues to be in a learning mode. The program staff developed an overview of the foundation's giving strategy, entitled *the Philanthropic Approach*, which has been reviewed by the Board. The Philanthropic Approach not only clearly defines the foundation's value and vision to "seek to exemplify the values and principles practiced by the foundation's founders: Integrity, Thinking Big, Humility, Stewardship and Compassion, but it also specifies priority program areas, establishes clear goals, and collaborates with partners to create coherent strategies to achieve those goals."[42]

Overall, the Hilton Foundation is aware of the importance of representing diverse populations, integrating into their priorities and practices the perspectives of the communities they exist to serve, and addressing the fundamental root causes of inequities. But, at a glance from the outside, this level of commitment is not readily apparent. It appears the foundation staff are dedicated to continuing on a journey to more deeply incorporate a commitment to DEI principles into all facets of the institution. As a foundation with significant global giving, it is also important to take into account the unique dimensions of demonstrating a commitment to constituent communities outside of the United States, particularly in Africa.

International Programming in Africa

All of the Hilton Foundation's international programs are in 17 countries in Africa and specifically focused on sub-Saharan Africa because the foundation wanted to rationalize resources and develop capacities. Due to the foundation's lean staff team, when it wants to engage substantively at a country-level, it can do only so much in a limited number of countries. Seventeen countries seem to be a fairly significant number of nations in which a U.S.-based foundation can be deeply engaged.

In addition to the grant making of various international foundations investing in Africa, philanthropy is growing in various African countries. However, local philanthropic infrastructure varies significantly from country to country in Africa. For example, Kenya has a 100-year history of philanthropy, while other countries such as Mali do not have developed Western-style philanthropic practices yet. According to Aid for Africa,[43] there are only a few charity organizations that work in Mali and most of them are grassroots organizations that work with African partners to help children and communities. "Philanthropy doesn't have to look like American foundations; it comes in many forms", says Kassim-Lakha, "We are trying to be quite conscious of that and showcase some of these other models of philanthropy and see how we give local philanthropy a voice in rolling out the SDGs and how do they begin to interface with these larger organizations."[44]

Launched in 2011, Young Children Affected by HIV and AIDS is one of the foundation's program areas in which much of the work is concentrated in Africa. The foundation focused on funding in five countries: Kenya, Mozambique, Malawi, Tanzania, and Zambia. MEL partners conducted an assessment of the foundation's work in these nations, and concluded that the Hilton Foundation knew how many children they touched, although the effects of these interventions are less understood. For instance, the Human Sciences Research Council (HSRC) in South Africa has provided a Monitoring, Evaluation and Learning (MEL) platform for the foundation's Young Children Affected by HIV and AIDS program area via a contract signed in November 2012. According to the report by HSRC[45] that evaluates the program, some of the foundation's achievements include, "leadership and leverage, opening up a new area and generating international and national interest in the work; the partnerships it has established with many of the largest and most experienced implementers of programs for children and communities affected by HIV and AIDS in sub-Saharan Africa."[46] The report also identified some of the program's deficiencies and suggested that "The foundation should further identify the niche it wants to occupy, and the areas in which it will continue to lead."[47]

Due to the MEL partner's engagement with local actors, the Hilton Foundation has transitioned to emphasize not only children's survival but their ability to survive and thrive. According to the foundation's report on improving the growth and development outcomes for young children affected by HIV and AIDS in East and Southern Africa, "The foundation would make investments to strengthen research and technical capacity – including for advancing measurement of child development outcomes." The foundation would also adopt "Field-testing approaches and reaching decision makers with evidence on what works will facilitate replication, scale-up and increased funding for quality early childhood services."[48] Following that transition, the World Health Organization (WHO) adopted a framework modeled after the Hilton Foundation's conclusions. As reported by the foundation, it is a "significant victory for global adoption of ECD (early childhood development, which is the focus of the foundation's Young Children Affected by HIV and AIDS program) practices when the World Health Organization launched the Nurturing Care Framework for Early Childhood Development."[49]

The foundation also plays significant roles in countries with established NGO and local philanthropic infrastructure. In the case of Kenya, the SDG Philanthropy Platform is cooperating with the local government in implementing SDGs. In this instance, the foundation and the platform are recognized as key allies of the government. "The workshops brought together representatives from philanthropy, governments, and the United Nations, to identify country-specific opportunities to collaborate on achieving global development goals." Through, as Kassim-Lakha says, "creating a space for local philanthropy to rally around is one of the key functions of the network and platform, and it is critical to paying attention to the idea of local giving. In developing the localized structures in various parts in Africa, one of the challenges of development is what metrics to use. It is better to use the SDGs so it is easier to rally everyone around that instead of crafting a unique set of metrics for one foundation."[50]

Measuring, Assessing Impact and Challenges in the Future

A commitment to learning from the perspectives of grantee and grantee constituent populations requires engagement – various mechanisms to listen to communities. Assessment is also an important feature in helping to understand the impact of foundations' investments on intended beneficiary populations. Ideally, efforts to solicit input from these populations influence programming and ultimately this improves impact. In the Hilton Foundation's international programming, continuous assessment has been gathering insights from grantees, which has influenced some change in program priorities.

Over a decade the foundation has had MEL partners (mostly third-party consultants) go out into communities to do primary research. They answer the question of how effective the five-year programmatic strategies have been on an annual basis. As outsiders, MEL partners seek to determine if the foundation has the right grantees in the portfolio and if it has made progress against the goals and objectives that were stated at the outset of the program's five-year strategy. While they aren't evaluating performance on a grantee-by-grantee level basis (that's the job of the foundation), they are doing high-level analysis across all of the grantees in a portfolio. They conduct a two-hour interview with grantees, speaking to community members, and gathering the information that helps the Hilton Foundation do better work and communicate with its grantees more effectively. MEL partners have been enabling the foundation to incorporate feedback from constituents to inform strategy for quite some time. The foundation's earliest project assessment could be traced back to 2007 when a preliminary assessment of WAWI (the West Africa Water Initiative) was done by an individual Nancy J. Allen based on documents' reviewing and interviews. Overall, these MEL partners have been providing important feedback on Hilton's current and future work.

When asked to reflect upon the impact of the foundation's international grantmaking approaches, Kassim-Lakha suggested that the foundation would probably need a longer time horizon in which to assess what has worked. She also indicated that what is not working well is the definition of philanthropy.[51] "For example, in some countries, the foundation is considered to be an international NGO; while in other countries, they are considered philanthropy because they are distributing grants; in Kenya, the foundation is viewed either a funder or a grantee, and that gets very murky in this field", says Kassim-Lakha.[52]

When discussing the future of international programs in a few years, Kassim-Lakha, mentioned that the foundation would i) work with local communities that can actually own the programs; ii) have measurable impacts on people's lives through the foundation's systems change, for which the foundation is putting all the bricks in place to work on at the moment; iii) have to make sure it is not just short-term funding that comes in to alleviate the problem.[53]

In terms of the foundation's ability to achieve its international programmatic goals, the concerns are mainly about financing. The foundation has been experimenting with alternative financing mechanisms such as water credit funds, development impact bond in Cameroon, etc. When the foundation is focusing on systems change, as Kassim-Lakha says, "it is challenging to make sure that the most vulnerable get what they need."[54] Overall, the international programs are in line with the core values of the foundation, which are thinking expansively, especially across cultures and a commitment to learning. The willingness to reflect on how the foundation serves its constituent populations in Africa and listen to local perspectives is an important reflection of the sense of responsibility the Hilton Foundation feels toward the nations in which they work. They also realize that there is much work to be done in order to enhance their impact in these communities as well as develop the broader institutional infrastructure demonstrating the values intended to drive programming and external engagement.

Notes

1 (Johnston and Delugach 1986)
2 (Conrad N Hilton, *History*, 2019)
3 (ProPublica 2019a)
4 (Walker and Siddique 2019)
5 (*Los Angeles Business Journal* 2017)
6 (Conrad N. Hilton Foundation, *Annual Report*, 2016)
7 (Conrad N. Hilton Foundation, *Grants*, 2019)
8 (Conrad N. Hilton Foundation, *Fast Facts*, 2019)

9 (Foundation Center and the Council on Foundations 2018)

10 (Interview, Cain 2018)

11 Ibid.

12 "The 2030 Agenda for Sustainable Development, adopted by all United Nations Member States in 2015, provides a shared blueprint for peace and prosperity for people and the planet, now and into the future. At its heart are the 17 Sustainable Development Goals (SDGs), which are an urgent call for action by all countries – developed and developing – in a global partnership. They recognize that ending poverty and other deprivations must go hand-in-hand with strategies that improve health and education, reduce inequality, and spur economic growth – all while tackling climate change and working to preserve our oceans and forests." (United Nations, *Sustainable Development Goals*, 2015)

13 Council on Foundations is founded in 1949, and is a nonprofit leadership association of grantmaking foundations and corporations. It provides the opportunity, leadership, and tools needed by philanthropic organizations to expand, enhance and sustain their ability to advance the common good. (From Council on Foundations, *About the Council*, 2019)

14 (Interview, Cain 2018)

15 Ibid.

16 "Mark Kramer is the co-founder and managing director of FSG and the author of influential publications on shared value, corporate social responsibility (CSR), catalytic philanthropy, strategic evaluation, impact investing and adaptive leadership." (Global Philanthropy Forum, *People – Mark Kramer*, 2019)

17 (Conrad N. Hilton Foundation, *Philanthropic Approach: How We Do It*, 2019)

18 "SDG Philanthropy Platform is a multi-year initiative led by the United Nations Development Programme (UNDP), the Foundation Center and Rockefeller Philanthropy Advisors (RPA), with funding support also from the MasterCard Foundation, Ford Foundation and others to draw awareness to and advocate for philanthropic engagement with the SDGs. The Hilton Foundation has invested nearly $10 million in grants over the past three years to promote collaboration advancing the SDGs, and the first investment was in the Post-2015 Partnership Platform." (Cain 2016)

19 (Interview, Kassim-Lakha 2018)

20 "IRC was founded in 1968 under an agreement between the World Health Organization and the Government of the Netherlands as a hub for information dissemination, a 'knowledge broker'. We were the focal point of a world-wide network of collaborating institutions active in water supply research and development." (IRC, *About Us*, 2019)

21 "As a strategic grantmaker, we rigorously analyze impact and lessons from our strategic initiatives to help inform our own work and that of other stakeholders. Working with external partners – for instance, a university or consultant team – the monitoring, evaluation and learning (MEL) process informs us of progress and challenges, so we can adjust our projects accordingly and share lessons learned with the sector in real-time." (Conrad N. Hilton Foundation, *Learning*, 2019)

22 (Interview, Kassim-Lakha 2018)

23 (Interview, Cain 2018)

24 Ibid.

25 Ibid.

26 (Conrad N. Hilton Foundation, *About Us – History*, 2019)

27 (Conrad N. Hilton Foundation, *Philanthropic Approach: How We Do It*, 2019)

28 (Conrad N. Hilton Foundation, *People – Board of Directors*, 2019)

29 (Interview, Cain 2018)

30 (Conrad N. Hilton Foundation, News on July 3 2019)

31 (Conrad N. Hilton Foundation, *People – Shaheen Kassim-Lakha*, 2019)

32 (Interview, Kassim-Lakha 2018)

33 (Conrad N. Hilton Foundation, *People – President and CEO*, 2019)

34 (Interview, Cain 2018)
35 Ibid.
36 Ibid.
37 Ibid.
38 Ibid.
39 Ibid.
40 (Interview, Ho 2018)
41 Ibid.
42 (Conrad N. Hilton Foundation, *Philanthropic Approach: Our Vision and Values*, 2019)
43 (Aid for Africa 2019)
44 (Interview, Kassim-Lakha 2018)
45 (Human Sciences Research Council 2016)
46 Ibid.
47 Ibid.
48 (Conrad N. Hilton Foundation, *2017–2021 Young Children Affected by HIV and AIDS Strategy,* 2017)
49 (Conrad N. Hilton Foundation, *Message from Peter Laugharn: Embracing the Global Revolution in Early Childhood Development*, 2018)
50 (Interview, Kassim-Lakha 2018)
51 Ibid.
52 Ibid.
53 Ibid.
54 Ibid.

References

Aid for Africa. *Charity Organizations that work in Mali.* 2019. https://www.aidforafrica. org/?cat=117&type=member-charities (accessed April 30, 2019).

Cain, Ed. Interview with David Maurrasse. Telephone Interview Recording. New York, April 5, 2018.

Cain, Ed. Why U.S. foundations should take the global Sustainable Development Goals seriously. 2016. https://www.hiltonfoundation.org/news/146-why-u-s-foundations-should-take-the-global-sustainable-development-goals-seriously (accessed March 6, 2019).

Conrad N. Hilton Foundation. *About – History.* 2019. https://www.hiltonfoundation. org/about/history (accessed April 20, 2019).

Conrad N. Hilton Foundation. *About Us – History.* 2019https://www.hiltonfoundation. org/about/history (accessed April 24, 2019).

Conrad N. Hilton Foundation. *Annual Report.* 2016. https://hilton-production.s3. ama zonaws.com/documents/274/attachments/2016__Statement_of_Financial_Position.pdf? 1502461993 (accessed April 2, 2019).

Conrad N. Hilton Foundation. *Grants.* 2019. https://www.hiltonfoundation.org/grants? priority=&geographic_area=usa&year=#filters (accessed April 2, 2019).

Conrad N. Hilton Foundation. *Fast Facts.* 2019. https://www.hiltonfoundation.org/about/ overview (accessed July 30, 2019).

Conrad N. Hilton Foundation. *Learning.* 2019. https://www.hiltonfoundation.org/lea rning?page=4&priority=&type=monitoring-evaluation-learning&year= (accessed April 29, 2019).

Conrad N. Hilton Foundation. Message from Peter Laugharn: Embracing the global revolution in early childhood development. 2018. https://www.hiltonfoundation.

org/news/303-message-from-peter-laugharn-embracing-the-global-revolution-in-ea rly-childhood-development (accessed April 30, 2019).

Conrad N. Hilton Foundation. News on July 3 2019: *The Conrad N. Hilton Foundation Announces Shaheen Kassim-Lakha as Director of Strategic Partnerships.* 2019. https://www.hil tonfoundation.org/news/445-the-conrad-n-hilton-foundation-announces-shaheen-kassim -lakha-as-director-of-strategic-partnerships (accessed April 24, 2019).

Conrad N. Hilton Foundation. *Philanthropic Approach: How We Do It.* 2019. https://www. hiltonfoundation.org/philanthropic-approach-how-we-do-it (accessed March 4, 2019).

Conrad N. Hilton Foundation. *Philanthropic Approach: How We Do It.* 2019https://www. hiltonfoundation.org/philanthropic-approach-how-we-do-it (accessed April 29, 2019).

Conrad N. Hilton Foundation. *Philanthropic Approach: Our Vision and Values.* 2019. https:// www.hiltonfoundation.org/philanthropic-approach (accessed April 24, 2019).

Conrad N. Hilton Foundation. *People – Board of Directors.* 2019https://www.hiltonfounda tion.org/people/departments/board-of-directors (accessed April 24, 2019).

Conrad N. Hilton Foundation. *People – Shaheen Kassim-Lakha, DrPH.* 2019. https://www. hiltonfoundation.org/people/shaheen-kassim-lakha (accessed April 24, 2019).

Conrad N. Hilton Foundation. *People – President and CEO.* 2019. https://www.hilton foundation.org/people/peter-laugharn (accessed April 24, 2019).

Conrad N. Hilton Foundation. *2017–2021 Young Children Affected by HIV and AIDS Strategy.* 2017. https://hilton-production.s3.amazonaws.com/documents/294/attachm ents/2017-2021_YCABA_Strategy_Overview_Document.pdf?1525449699 (accessed April 30, 2019).

Council on Foundations. *About the Council.* 2019. https://www.cof.org/about (accessed April 30, 2019).

Foundation Center and the Council on Foundations. *The State of Global Giving by U.S. Foundations 2011–2015.* 2018. https://www.issuelab.org/resources/31306/31306.pdf (accessed March 4, 2019).

Global Philanthropy Forum. *People – Mark Kramer.* 2019. https://philanthropyforum.org/p eople/mark-kramer/ (accessed April 19, 2019).

Ho, Jennifer. Interview with David Maurrasse and Joey DeMarco. Video Interview Recording. New York, April 5, 2018.

Human Sciences Research Council. *Evaluation of the Conrad N. Hilton Foundation's Initiative on Young Children Affected by HIV and AIDS Final Report.* 2016. https://hilton-produc tion.s3.amazonaws.com/documents/205/attachments/HSRC-Hilton_Foundation_Final _Report_Reduced_Secured.pdf?1462928229 (accessed April 30, 2019).

IRC. *About Us.* 2019. https://www.ircwash.org/about (accessed April 24, 2019).

Johnston, David and Al Delugach. Fight over Conrad Hilton estate gets increasingly bitter. *Los Angeles Times.* 1986. http://articles.latimes.com/1986-03-04/business/fi-15184_1_ conrad-hilton/ (accessed April 20, 2019).

Los Angeles Business Journal. Wealthiest Angelenos: 12. William Barron Hilton. 2017. http://labusinessjournal.com/news/2017/aug/24/wealthiest-angelenos-12-william-ba rron-hilton/ (accessed April 21, 2019).

Kassim-Lakha, Shaheen. Interview with David Maurrasse and Joey DeMarco. Video Interview Recording. New York, March 9, 2018.

ProPublica. *Conrad N Hilton Foundation. 2009 Form 990-PF.* 2019a. https://projects.prop ublica.org/nonprofits/display_990/943100217/2010_11_PF%2F94-3100217_990PF_ 200912 (accessed April 20, 2019).

ProPublica. *Conrad N Hilton Foundation. Nonprofit Explorer: Research Tax-Exempt Organizations.* 2019b. https://projects.propublica.org/nonprofits/organizations/943100217 (accessed April 20, 2019).

United Nations. *Sustainable Development Goals.* 2015. https://sustainabledevelopment.un. org/sdgs (accessed April 25, 2019).

Walker, Peter and Haroon Siddique. Hilton grandfather pledges fortune to charity. *The Guardian.* 2007. https://www.theguardian.com/world/2007/dec/27/usa.haroonsiddi que (accessed April 21, 2019).

6

FAMILY PHILANTHROPY

Mary Reynolds Babcock Foundation

Background on the Foundation

The Mary Reynolds Babcock Foundation (MRBF) is a family foundation in North Carolina founded in 1953. The foundation has always been committed to concepts such as equity and social justice. The foundation was originally established with a $12 million bequest from Mary Reynolds Babcock in order to support historically black colleges and universities, grassroots advocacy groups, voter education and government accountability efforts. The foundation funds throughout the American South (in 11 states), maintaining a particular commitment to a broad, diverse, and complex geographical region. With over US$176.4 million in assets, giving away $7.1 million for 2016, the foundation helps dollars stretch a long way in order to improve Southern communities. As stated in the foundation's mission statement, "the Babcock Foundation's mission is to help people and places move out of poverty and achieve greater social and economic justice." In late 2016, the foundation revamped its strategic direction to be more equity-focused.

Over the years, the foundation has made numerous grants in areas of economic opportunity (such as job training, education, connection to employers and entrepreneurship), democracy and civic engagement (such as community planning and development, leadership development) and supportive policies and institutions. Since 2016, about 100 grants were made to various funds and organizations aligned with the foundation's mission.

MRBF is more than a grantmaking institution. It is increasingly a civic actor – a catalyst to encourage greater action in communities. The foundation is building partnerships in various Southern localities in order to encourage and expand networks. More recently, it concluded that it could make the greatest impact, with its limited dollars, by leveraging resources from elsewhere in addition to making grants. Justin Maxson, the foundation's Director has experienced MRBF from the point of view of a grantee as well. While he is relatively new to MRBF as an executive, he led a grantee organization for 15 years.

MRBF's Board operates in ten-year cycles. In their last ten-year arc, the foundation focused on asset development, funding organizations such as Community Development Financial Institutions (CDFIs). Recently, they reflected at the end of the last ten-year period, and chose a different direction. He said of the most recent shift, "We stepped back from this focus because our experience says we should support networks of groups working across strategies."[1] Because the foundation stressed listening to grantees and the communities in which they are situated, MRBF witnessed the value of collaboration across community-based organizations as an important aspect of facilitating change in geographic places. Maxson continued, "The foundation is issue agnostic, because what is most important is the alignment of groups in a place – could be around economic development, civic engagement, any issue... It is about constellations of groups figuring out how to be powerful together."[2]

In focusing on community change, the foundation was willing to remain open and observe the scenario in the various Southern States the foundation prioritizes. Remaining open without asking grantees to fit into its pre-established conclusions, MRBF found itself transcending issues. Most foundation programming is structured around particular issues, accompanied by specific guidelines within each issue area. This foundation is taking a broader view. Maxson realizes that an emphasis on networks requires a particular set of roles for MRBF. The role far exceeds that of a grantmaker, only giving away money. This focus on multiple organizations collaborating on numerous interconnected issues facing specific geographic areas requires a foundation to wear multiple hats. For Maxson, this comprehensive role begins with respecting the voices in the communities they hope to improve. He said, "We recognize that the groups on the ground know better. We engage communities about their perspective on the needs; and the foundation brings multiple tools to the work. We help networks raise other funds. We try to broker relationships for local partners. The foundation helps connect the dots. We also bring PRIs and MRIs[3] – all in response to how communities want to work in their places. Place helps us understand one's context. There are multiple 'Souths' – urban and rural. The rural south is not homogenous either. Being place-based helps us get a better handle on the issues."[4]

MRBF helps raise money, build partnerships, and bring other resources to the table by leveraging investment income. This is an active role for a foundation. But, because of MRBF's emphasis on listening to communities, grantees and grantees' constituents play a role in shaping the foundation's strategic direction. They are also aware of the range of distinct contexts amongst the various Southern States in which they work. They can only effectively understand each of these places if they are engaged within them. Understanding each of these places helps the foundation target their efforts and recognize the role they should play to advance grantees' collective action.

This is today's MRBF. It is a foundation driven by values and a willingness to adapt to experiences in the communities they prioritize. This organization happens to be a family foundation with living family members who remain active on the Board. MRBF's high level of community engagement is not characteristic of most family foundations.

Considerations for the Particular Type of Foundation

As philanthropic organizations, which are an extension of the wishes of family members, family foundations experience unique dynamics and circumstances. Very particular desires of specific family members and family politics can shape the nature and impact of these unique forms of institutional philanthropy. These peculiarities are often manifested in Boards of Trustees. Typically, the Boards of family foundation are comprised mostly of family members, who may or may not have expertise in the foundation's substantive areas of interest. MRBF was intentional from the beginning about including nonfamily members, who have expertise in the nature of the foundation's work.

Laura Mountcastle is a second-generation family member who has been on the Board since the mid 1980s. She reflected on the evolution of the inclusion of nonfamily Board members, "We have had nonfamily board members bringing expertise in different areas. In the early 1990s, we emphasized bringing more diversity to the board – in expertise, region, race, and people who are on the ground working in the community. Some were grassroots and some were academic. Even the academics were people who were studying the region."[5] But the foundation remains committed to incorporating family members on the Board regardless of their particular interests or experiences. All of Laura's generation were invited to join the Board, for example. Nonfamily members are on the Board for three-year, renewable terms.

Of invitations to family members to join the Board, Mountcastle said, "All of the family members (five grandkids) accepted the invitation. Three of them are still on the Board. But, there are 11 in the next generation. How will this affect mission and values?"[6] This is the inherent complexity in family foundations. In the case of MRBF, a continued dedication to including family members co-exists with the inclusion of nonfamily members. To date, it appears this has been a harmonious relationship that has enhanced the foundation's work. Going forward, the balance could shift. No one can guarantee that all family members will share the same values as new family members continue to accept invitations to the Board.

The Board is continually thinking through how to remain a family foundation while representing the communities the foundation serves. Mountcastle discussed how the foundation has continued to recruit new members and consider gaps to be filled. She said, "We have three new Board members. We bring in Board members reflecting regions where we are doing work. If someone from Georgia is leaving the Board, we want to add someone from that region. We are also looking to get younger people on the Board."[7] The foundation has been deliberately nominating and recruiting Board members that will help them include wide representation across Southern communities. The foundation's experiences have demonstrated the functional value of inclusion at the Board level, as it has been shaping strategic priorities.

Maxson points to the longstanding commitment to certain values in the family and among the entire Board as a crucial reason he took on the executive leadership of the foundation. He reflected on the evolution of the Board's thinking and composition, "There was a baked inset of values in the family – equity, justice, democracy. These values were core to the early set of family members that created the foundation. The first 20 years, there was a broad base of family interests. The middle 20 years saw an increasing sense of strategy creating programs about democracy. In the third 20 years, the family turned to strategic philanthropy. They focused on bringing on nonfamily members to the Board. They wanted the Board to reflect the communities they care about – people of color, those who have had experience with poverty. There was a desire for greater impact and shifting the culture of the Board."[8]

Over the years, this commitment to including nonfamily experts has remained and evolved. The nature of desired expertise and demographics of expert Board members has changed. Otis Johnson is a longtime nonfamily Board member. Johnson is from Savannah, Georgia. He is the former Mayor of the City. When he first joined the MRBF Board, he was leading a community-based initiative, the Youth Futures Authority. He first joined the Board in 1996. He was brought onto the Board with another new member in order to bring different perspectives from the communities the foundation represents. This recruitment of nonfamily members was intended to incorporate viewpoints that would help them add value to their work in Southern communities. Recalling his initial interview process with the foundation, Johnson stated, "I told them that they could not do the work they were committing to do with a Board and staff that looked like their Board and staff."[9] Evidently, this perspective shared during the interview did not deter the foundation from asking him to join. This is the kind of candor they were seeking.

But bringing on an African American community leader from Georgia, such as Dr. Johnson is only one step. Genuinely including his voice in decision making over his tenure on the Board is the greater challenge. Regarding this dynamic, Johnson indicated, "There are more nonfamily members on the Board than family members now; and we are fully embraced. This is a result of their values. They really embrace values that I would like to see be the driving force in all organizations. The family practices what they preach."[10] He continued with respect to how the relationship between family and nonfamily Board members is manifested in deliberations. He said, "There have not been any times that any family member tried to remind non-family Board members of a difference in authority and involvement. The same is true in reviewing grants."[11] Johnson is referring to highly relevant dynamics on family foundation Boards and in philanthropy in general. The sources of money in philanthropy – the donors – have control. It is up to donors to determine how they want to exercise the inherent power that comes with possessing large sums of money to distribute. These circumstances are particularly apparent when living donors interface with Board and staff decision makers in foundations. This is a part of what makes family foundations intriguing.

In many ways, family foundations are microcosms of philanthropy as a whole. They involve wealth possessed by donors to be distributed in the form of grants to support various causes. But, because the money is theirs, they have the latitude to decide how this funding will be spent, whether or not this spending is in the best interests of the communities they intend to serve. In order to alter this arrangement, a conscious effort is required to create new mechanisms to enhance the responsiveness of family foundations to communities – to society. In the case of MRBF, the incorporation of nonfamily Board members representing Southern communities *and* the willingness to listen to their viewpoints in decision making represents an approach to revise the dynamic. This approach builds new bridges to the community and enables nonfamily perspectives to inform the foundation's priorities. This technique is also cognizant of race and other demographics in building a more representative Board.

It is also important to note that despite the challenges inherent in the structure of family foundations, this kind of philanthropic institution is the most common. According to the foundation Stats by Foundation Center,[12] in 2014 the U.S. had 42,008 family foundations, which accounted for 48.4% of all the 86,726 foundations nationwide. With this significant number and a range of endemic characteristics, family foundations require focused attention. Exponent Philanthropy is an association, which has been addressing family foundations' needs. Two decades ago, the Association of Small Foundations (ASF) was founded and later became Exponent Philanthropy, which is now the "largest philanthropic support organization in the country and the only one dedicated to serving funders who give with few or no staff."[13]

Strategy – The Essence of the Foundation's Strategy

As noted, every ten years, the foundation steps back and reflects on its impact and relevance. Recently, the foundation underwent such a process. The foundation's mission remains the same. But every ten years, the foundation refines its strategy, informed by a process that includes listening to community voices. They hire a consultant to conduct interviews with grantees and other external constituents. The most recent strategic planning process informed the aforementioned emphasis on networks.

According to Maxson, the strategy is "more of a compass than a map."[14] The foundation did not design a rigid strategic plan with specific outcomes over a particular period of time. Maxson continued, "We have a set of strategic directions… If we had a rigid strategic plan in place a couple of years ago, it would not have worked. We have increased civic engagement spending because of the elections."[15] It is clear from this perspective that the foundation has moved away from the characteristics that are typically associated with strategic philanthropy, which emphasizes sharp focus driving toward specific results. The MRBF's emphasis on networks is informed by engagement in the communities they have been funding. They realize that the challenges confronting low income people and communities of color in the South are shaped by numerous contextual dynamics, such as politics, which significantly transcend the targeted results of singular organizations on short-term grants. Greater civic participation in these communities would help community residents play a greater role in influencing elections in policies in their cities and states. Consequently, the foundation is shifting toward this broader focus on civic engagement.

The foundation's strategic direction does not highlight particular issue areas. However, it includes three broad pathways. Maxson said, "The strategic directions approach has served us well. As we developed our plan, we focused on multiple strategies – lifted up supportive institution, policy change and civic engagement. The staff is more attuned to these three main pathways. We are looking for networks that are working across these three pathways. We had to be on this path already in order to address post-election period."[16] The 2016 elections stimulated significant reflection among many organizations and communities. In the case of MRBF, it recognized the need to invest in influencing the policies affecting its target communities, affect the ways in which these communities vote, and to remain a foundation that is supportive of community organizations and cognizant of their contexts.

The foundation is also continually considering ways to harness additional resources to complement its grantmaking as a small foundation. This has led the foundation to reflect on how it approaches its legally required 5% annual spending. Maxson indicated, "We increased our spending policy beyond 5%. We added a percent. And then the Board said 'It's not enough'."[17] For Otis Johnson, maximizing impact despite their stature is a Board priority. He declared, "MRBF is a small organization; so we have to maximize impact. If we increase economic opportunity and increase civic engagement and build supportive policies and institutions, then we will get greater impact in moving communities out of poverty and increasing opportunities. This has come from years of reflection and including grantees in the thinking."[18] Johnson references both the nature of their work as well as the process that infused the strategy with grantee perspectives. He went further, indicating a multi-layered approach that includes supporting networks of organizations. He stated, "We emphasize place-based interventions. But we also support collaboratives, which increases our impact. If a collaborative is working with ten or 15 groups, we are increasing our impact."[19] Clearly a part of their learning is that funding singular organizations will get them only so far if altering life opportunities for lower income communities is central to their vision. They intentionally support clusters of organizations. This conclusion reflects some of their learning from continued engagement with grantees and grantee constituent communities.

Laura Mountcastle suggests the foundation's mission has been consistent, but its strategy evolves as it continually adapt based on learning. She said, "Our mission is to move people out of poverty and get social and economic justice. The mission is consistent, but we are doing more on democracy and civic engagement and economic opportunity and supportive policies and institutions."[20] The foundation's approach has changed. With a broad mission focusing on ending poverty and pursuing social and economic justice, the actual role and impact of a single relatively small family foundation would have to be somewhat targeted and include activities that stretch dollars a long way. Policy change, for example, is one way in which smaller investments could influence broader impact in communities.

In developing a strategy, a foundation must not only consider the substance of programming, but tactical ways to make grants and leverage resources beyond grantmaking budgets. Mountcastle points to some ways in which they have been harnessing their dollars. She said, "General support and longer-term commitments are helpful for partners in trying to get the work done. We are using financial assets for grants and program related investments. We are becoming more strategic about our financial assets."[21] It is clear that the leadership of MRBF is focused on impact in communities, and willing to review varying potential approaches. The foundation is investing in networks with more flexible and longer-term grants. They are also making greater use of their assets beyond dollars designated for grantmaking.

Commitment to Equity and Inclusion – The Foundation's Overall Commitment to Inclusion

Inclusion is at the heart of the foundation's current strategic approach, as it emphasizes the perspectives of those in the communities MRBF is funding. Maxson experienced this as a grantee, and recognizes the depth of effort required to truly engage and learn from communities. He reflected, "This is a challenging form of grantmaking that involves generalists and an ability to bring trust. In order to get to authentic voices, we have to build trust in local partners across the South, which is a big, diverse place."[22] Maxson speaks to a couple of important dynamics that surface in philanthropy. First of all, there are many barriers to true authenticity in foundation/grantee relations. Grantees are often placed in a position of filtering out some of the most challenging aspects of their work to avoid seeming like failures and losing their funding. How can a grantee trust a funder to the point where he/she are comfortable sharing fully? This cannot happen instantly. It takes time. Maxson refers to the process of building trust. This is the reality of foundation/grantee communication. It takes time to establish mutual trust. Secondly, Maxson speaks to the importance of context – the diversity of geographical contexts within the one large region the foundation supports. Authentically understanding each of these contexts requires a presence in these areas, and true engagement.

Communication between grantees and foundations is often about grantees making a case to foundations in order to match a funder's stated areas of interest. Sometimes this communication may exaggerate the significance and potential of an organization's work. Indeed, this dynamic can be influenced by a culture in philanthropy that stresses achieving unrealistic results in short periods of time. This tendency can lead to overpromising and downplaying the magnitude of work required to achieve a certain set of results. MRBF seeks to depart from these patterns. Maxson said, "Hyperbole is not the way for a grantee to sell the MRBF. MRBF understands the work and spends time building trust."[23] He continued, "Growing an understanding of the place is central to our approach. We focus on long-term general support – seven or more years. A real relationship must be created."[24] The foundation does not encourage spinning to sell an organization's work. A relationship between the foundation and grantees is a goal. This relationship enables trust and honest communication about what it really takes in order to achieve complex community change. Instead of encouraging grantees to fit themselves into a narrow set of guidelines for a grant lasting a few months, MRBF engages in relationship-building toward long-term partnerships with grantees.

Bernie Mazyck is a current grantee. He is the President and CEO of the South Carolina Association for Community Economic Development (SCACED). He has been President and CEO of this organization for 24 years. SCACED is a coalition focused on building healthy and economically sustainable communities in South Carolina. The organization has had a relationship with MRBF for over 20 years. Mazyck has also experienced MRBF's deep engagement and genuine effort to be inclusive. He said that MRBF, "Intentionally works to ensure that they have representation from the most marginalized communities to frame and develop the strategies that they hold. These people have to have a place at the table. They are inclusive across the economic spectrum as well. Economic, racial, and gender equity are all important components of their work."[25] SCACED has over 100 members, which helps them collectively impact South Carolina communities. About half of their support has come from MRBF; and the foundation has leveraged additional resources for them as well. Mazyck has seen MRBF evolve over the years. And he has noticed the increased emphasis on networks. His characterizations of the foundation's current approach are as follows, "They recognized the need to grow a network of grassroots leaders in marginalized communities and grassroots communities, and allow those leaders to network with their colleagues. They were a facilitator, not only a funder of initiatives."[26]

MRBF's intended approach is recognized by a grantee. He sees how networks have become increasingly significant in the foundation's work. He also notices its role beyond making grants. In many ways, MRBF is a change agent, helping to convene the networks of those who should collaborate in order to influence improvements in their communities. Mazyck has experienced MRBF's intentional effort to maximize the impact of grantees. He indicated, "MRBF has been critical in engaging local, state, and federal policymakers."[27] SCACED is an example of an organization that has received long-term unrestricted funding from MRBF, and has benefited from a close working relationship with the foundation.

This working relationship has opened additional doors for SCACED and expanded their influence and impact as an organization. MRBF's inclusiveness is manifested on a number of levels. The foundation has built in ongoing lines of communication with communities, included representation from these communities on the Board and staff, and developed deep ongoing partnerships with particular organizations representing these communities. All three of these areas enable insights and experiences from communities to inform and refine MRBF's strategic direction. In its partnerships with organizations such as SCACED, MRBF gains valuable knowledge and understanding about South Carolina communities, which enables the foundation to better recognize how it can have an impact through grants and otherwise. The multifaceted approach that MRBF has chosen − helping to create and sustain networks, making long-term unrestricted grants, leveraging funds from investments and elsewhere, harnessing partnerships with other funding agencies, and influencing local policy − all are guided by community perspectives. MRBF's ability to impact local communities has increased because of the depth of their engagement in communities in the South. This engagement along with the inclusion of appropriate representative voices in the organization has helped the foundation stretch well beyond how it made grants earlier in its history.

Manifestations of Commitment − Techniques and Practices

How Inclusion Informs Strategy Programmatically

MRBF is committed to values. Since the foundation's inception, values have informed practice and the evolution of the organization's policies and practices over time. Otis Johnson reflected on this, "We have a set of values that drive the work. Anything we do has to uphold these values. Because of this work, we are respected. We are in the South. And we are not afraid to confront the evils of poverty and racism and injustice."[28] For Johnson, the relationship between the foundation and grantees is crucial to MRBF's strategy and values. He said, "MRBF values the relationship; it is not top down. It is two-way. MRBF is not a charity. The attitude associated with philanthropy is not what it would embrace. MRBF knows in order to get to a strategic plan, it has to partner with grantees and other organizations."[29] He makes an important point in these remarks. He distinguishes between the "two-way" relationship to which MRBF aspires and the approach that he associates with "philanthropy". He demonstrates an awareness that their method of operating is not typical in "philanthropy" or "charity". A commitment to being responsive to communities, according to Johnson, is unusual for a family foundation.

This commitment is manifested in how the foundation approaches its grantees and grantee constituent communities. In their view, the communities know best. The foundation's strategy must be open to being informed by the communities. MRBF does not want to tell the community what to do. In terms of external engagement, the foundation stopped referring to their Grantmakers on staff as "Program Officers". They now refer to these program staff as "Network Officers", who are responsible for being engaged in the various neighborhoods across the South in which they have invested. These Officers are present in these communities in order to understand them and identify opportunities to leverage additional resources in support of their grantees.

As Maxson brings a grantee's perspective beyond his role as the foundation's Director, he recalled his experience on the other side of the foundation. He said, "I loved site visits from the foundation when I was a grantee. I had worked with 30 foundations. MRBF was the only one that sent questions ahead of time. This made us better at what we were doing."[30] This is an area where the foundation's firm belief that the communities know best was manifested in the grantee experience. It is interesting to hear a former grantee reflect on a site visit experience with such affection, as site visits are often nerve-wracking moments for many grantees in their interactions with their funders. Maxson experienced something more of a collaboration with the foundation when he was a grantee, which included continuous communication. He continued, "As a grantee, we co-created the work with MRBF. There was a series of conversations over a year. The Officer visited multiple times during the year. But she came down respectfully. MRBF always shows up with respect. The Network Officer asked hard questions about the work that never implied she was smarter."[31] Maxson's experiences reflected a collaborative approach, which seemed to de-emphasize the power dynamic between foundations and grantees. It appears MRBF created an atmosphere in which grantee perspectives were allowed to drive the relationship rather than vice versa. This is not a circumstance in which the foundation primarily told the grantee what to do.

For Mountcastle, listening to communities is fundamental to the foundation's methods. This helps the foundation understands how its role as a philanthropic organization can best target the core concerns facing the populations whose lives it hopes to improve. She said, "We have to understand we are working with low wealth people – the people being affected have to be a part of the solution and working on strategies and are a part of the process."[32] She also elaborated on the foundation's methods to engage communities, "There are formal and informal processes to listen to grantees. The Network Officers are good at asking grantees about what is going on in the communities. The Network Officers are able to identify those organizations that are genuinely reflective of local communities. The staff is intentional about who is at meetings – not only those who are at the top – also those who are the customers."[33] She makes the distinction between only hearing from the leaders of nonprofit organizations and getting to the perspectives of the community residents who are served by those organizations, who are the ultimate intended beneficiary populations. It is also important to highlight the idea of sorting out those organizations that are genuinely representing their communities versus others. This is a persistent challenge facing philanthropy – how to get beyond funding primarily organizations that are well-positioned and well-financed, but not necessarily engaged in the communities their work is designed to serve. It appears MRBF is very well aware of some of the ways in which historically disenfranchised communities have not been served adequately by the nonprofit sector.

How Inclusion Informs Strategy Institutionally

Once per year, the foundation connects the Board with grantees, traveling to a particular part of the South to hear from grantees directly.

From an institutional point of view, this has implications for who is on the staff and Board. The demographics and experiences of staff and Board matter in shaping how the foundation can carry out this community-engaged mission effectively. To a certain degree, the foundation must reflect the varying demographics of grantee communities. The CEO himself is a former longtime grantee of MRBF. Additionally, other demographics reflecting various Southern communities are represented throughout the organization.

The foundation requests demographic data from existing and prospective grantees. This information helps the foundation understand if these organizations are reflective of the communities in which they are working. Laura Mountcastle said, "In our applications, we ask about demographics in the Boards of organizations. In some areas, this type of diversity is harder to find – but we have to make sure that the composition is reflective of the place."[34] Furthermore, because MRBF includes Board members with experiences in various Southern communities, they can bring insights about particular organizations to help the foundation's decision making.

Mazyck, from a grantee's point of view, has noticed the intentional way in which MRBF has been inclusive institutionally. He said, "It is important not to overlook MRBF's commitment to equity and inclusion at the Board level and on the staff level. Both represent inclusion from a gender and minority perspective. I want to applaud MRBF for that – their rhetoric – and embedding what they're doing into the work."[35] From the outside, he can see that the foundation is living up to its values in practice.

The continued inclusion of nonfamily Board members has been an important demonstration of how voices more reflective of the communities the foundation funds are valued. These outside expert Board members have been instrumental in shaping the foundation's current direction. Otis Johnson said, "We have modeled our commitment in terms of our Board structure and the way the Board works."[36] The way the foundation incorporates nonfamily Board members and strives for diversity and inclusion on the Board is a reflection of values to Johnson. It is not perfect, and the situation continues to be a work in progress. Johnson said, "sometimes there is a gap between what we profess and what we do."[37] But, for the most part, he has seen the foundation live up to its values.

This is a departure from many family foundations, which can become pre-occupied with their own individual interests or the interests of ancestors over those of today's historically disenfranchised communities.

Progress – What Has Been the Impact of these Approaches? How Do They Measure Progress?

The foundation's current strategy is somewhat new. But they have already experienced the value of the foundation's ability to leverage additional opportunities. Mountcastle feels she has seen progress since she joined the Board. She stated, "Over the time I have been on the Board, the foundation has become more focused and strategic. We were funding everywhere; and it was hard to measure impact. We became more strategic – we measure grantee outcomes."[38] When asked what she has learned from her experiences on the Board, she replied, "The importance of diversity, and long-term commitment to grantees. We have some learning activities during all of our meetings. We bring in grantees and experts to share their knowledge. The voices of those affected need to be included."[39] The Board's ability to hear from communities supported by the foundation is built into the Board's experience. She continued, "Listening to the grantees is how we came to the conclusion of focusing on general operating support and long-term grants. Leadership development and capacity building was another important conclusion. We have an amazing staff that listens to communities."[40] Here again, it is clear that MRBF has institutionalized listening to the communities it supports. This is happening at the level of the staff and Board, and the foundation's leadership is allowing this engagement to define strategic directions.

MRBF measures impact by reviewing at different levels. As the foundation has been supporting networks, levels of impact are on numerous fronts. Mountcastle said of this multi-layered approach of assessing progress, "With data we have collected, we try to look at the network of grants. For each area, we have a rationale – is the organization effective, is the network effective, and is the overall region effective?"[41]

Maxson elaborated on the foundation's approach to evaluation. The foundation relies on, what it calls, *Rationales*. Maxson said, "*Rationales* define signs of progress in each place. We ask the grantees to tell us about their signs of progress. In Appalachia, for example, we have five signs of progress. These are indicators across the work."[42] MRBF, while having selected three broad areas to explore in their strategic direction, does have an approach to measuring progress. The foundation's place-based emphasis is very apparent in this assessment method. MRBF focuses on particular geographical areas in the South, helps build networks of organizations in these areas, and develops ideas about how to facilitate change in these regions based on the perspectives and experiences of residents and organizations in these areas.

The three pathways in the foundation's strategic direction frame these *Rationales.* Maxson continued, "*Rationales* identify signs of progress. We have three priorities – civic engagement, supportive policy, institutions. The changing context around the election, came afterward. It turns out that we were "better prepared" because we had been focused on multi-strategy networks. Better things happen when these networks with shared strategies are in place."[43] The reference to preparation in these remarks is intriguing. It appears the increased community capacity to advocate on its own behalf in various segments of the South is an important outcome of MRBF's strategic direction and emphasis on networks. They helped bring organizations together around common interests. The *Rationales* are internal, unpublished documents of four to six pages addressing qualitative and quantitative indicators on varying communities. According to Maxson, *Rationales* are summaries describing a place and progress in a place. Causality and attribution are very difficult in these documents. We emphasize MRBF's contribution to the communities where we are working. We are interested in the grantees' contributions. For us, this is not evaluation; it is learning. We do have hard conversations when we don't see outcomes. But, we are patient because we understand that the work is under resourced. We want to build the capacity of organizations led by people of color and serving communities that have been under resourced."[44]

Maxson speaks to some of philanthropy's persistent challenges, such as the complexity of attribution, the ability to recognize the realistic context facing grassroots organizations, the need for patience in organizations' ability to address difficult issues, and the importance of capacity building. In philanthropy, lofty ideas about community improvement and demonstrable change in crucial social and economic issues are confronted with various limitations. Organizations often do not have the resources to influence substantial changes, particularly in the short term. MRBF is expecting to see greater impact going forward because of their support of networks as well as their deeper understanding of the communities in which it works.

Conclusions, Lessons, and Directions

MRBF has continually evolved over generations through learning. They have proven to be a learning organization, which is continually reflecting and adapting. They have institutionalized moments to pause and assess their progress in the short and long terms.

When asked what he has learned from his experiences on the MRBF Board, Johnson answered, "That there is power and wisdom at the local level that needs to be harnessed and networked into larger efforts to bring about social change. In the building of these organizations and networks, they can leverage partnerships to do what they need to improve people and places who have been mired in poverty for generations and have been almost powerless."[45] This is the essence of what a small family foundation – the Mary Reynolds Babcock Foundation – is trying to achieve through a thoughtful application of dedication to improving Southern communities and a willingness to develop an agenda with community input.

Mountcastle feels the foundation has learned quite a bit recently. She said, "We have learned that layering and networks are ways of getting things done. We are looking at structural issues that are affecting low wealth communities – working at grassroots and grass-tops. We work with structures at the State levels that provide information to organizations – sources of strategy development – getting groups together. Voting rights – the structural systems that keep people from voting."[46] Remaining connected to the foundation's grantees and grantee constituent communities has helped inform a multi-faceted view of how MRBF can facilitate change in Southern communities. It is a matter of understanding the systemic ways in which communities are being affected, and employing a range of approaches to influence policy, voting rights, and other areas that are shaping the realities of lower income communities in the region. As she indicated, this approach is not only a matter of engaging communities at the grassroots level, it is also about the foundation's willingness to work at the "grass-tops". This means direct communication with public officials and other influential leaders positioned to change systems internally.

Going forward, the foundation intends to continue its current course of action, continually seeking new ways to leverage additional dollars and other resources in order to advance the efforts of their grantees and constituents. Mountcastle said of MRBF's direction, "We are in a stay the course mode, but we want to be more nimble. Civic engagement has become very important to us. We want to move more quickly and direct more funds in this area. We are looking with more intentionality around equity and inclusion and how we learn. We might do some Board work in this regard. We believe we have been equitable and inclusive, but we have to review our policies and practices."[47]

They have begun to pursue impact investing as one evolving approach to stretch their assets beyond grantmaking.

Partnerships are going to become increasingly significant in the foundation's strategic approach. Otis Johnson looks ahead, "We are going to continue working on our layering strategies. There is no one approach or silver bullet to reducing poverty or increasing equality in the South or anywhere. We are looking to develop complementary strategies that build on the learning we get from places and other organizations. We have to keep learning how to do this work better. To change the South, it will take multiple decades of hard, focused work on reducing the structural barriers that keep people in poverty. We are looking to use grants and PRIs to do what they can do best to leverage resources – network with other organizations. We want to increase the capacity of grassroots organizations. We are looking at policies at State levels that are preventing communities from getting better. We have been traveling down this road for a few years."[48] Evidently, the future of MRBF is multi-faceted. The foundation realizes that it can only achieve its mission with a broader menu of options from strengthening singular organizations, to investing in networks of organizations, to influencing statewide policies, to leveraging their other assets via program-related investments.

These approaches allow MRBF to do more than their assets as a family foundation would suggest. For Maxson, the ability to leverage resources from elsewhere on behalf of grantees is paramount. He said, "We are looking for ways to punch above our weight class."[49] He also sees needs for growth in the foundation's ability to learn, perhaps by adding staff focused specifically on assessment and learning. He also added, "We are trying to get clearer about how equity impacts our grantmaking. The racial wealth gap and how to build coalitions of people of color and white communities are important as well."[50]

Overall, MRBF is a compelling example of a family foundation, which has continually reflected on its value and impact as a way to increase its value to Southern communities. It has allowed its strategy development and implementation to be informed by grantees and grantee constituent communities in a way that transcends most family foundations. They have constructed institutional techniques to ensure that community voices are adequately incorporated. This intention to include community perspectives is viewed by MRBF as a path toward greater impact. Listening to community voices allowed them to recognize the value of networks in solving problems at the community level. While MRBF has not been funding with this particular point of view for very long, it is already seeing the potential value of this approach. The Foundation is actively seeking to be a valuable resource for Southern communities, which can not only make grants, but seek to understand their needs and leverage additional resources to meet them. In this regard, an inclusive approach both informed the foundation's strategic direction and helped shape a range of techniques that are expanding resources to Southern communities. In this sense, MRBF is a better foundation. As a result of purposeful inclusion, the foundation is beginning to see impact, and positioning its work to influence even greater improvements in the neighborhoods and regions it emphasizes.

Notes

1 (Interview, Maxson 2018)
2 Ibid.
3 "Program-Related Investments" and "Mission-Related Investments"
4 (Interview, Maxson 2018)
5 (Interview, Mountcastle 2018)
6 Ibid.

7 Ibid.
8 (Interview, Maxson 2018)
9 (Interview, Johnson 2018)
10 Ibid.
11 Ibid.
12 (Foundation Center 2019)
13 (Exponent Philanthropy 2019)
14 (Interview, Maxson 2018)
15 Ibid.
16 Ibid.
17 Ibid.
18 (Interview, Johnson 2018)
19 Ibid.
20 (Interview, Mountcastle 2018)
21 Ibid.
22 (Interview, Maxson 2018)
23 Ibid.
24 Ibid.
25 (Interview, Mazyck 2018)
26 Ibid.
27 Ibid.
28 (Interview, Johnson 2018)
29 Ibid.
30 (Interview, Maxson 2018)
31 Ibid.
32 (Interview, Mountcastle 2018)
33 ibid
34 ibid
35 (Interview, Mazyck 2018)
36 (Interview, Johnson 2018)
37 Ibid.
38 (Interview, Mountcastle 2018)
39 Ibid.
40 Ibid.
41 Ibid.
42 (Interview, Maxson 2018)
43 Ibid.
44 Ibid.
45 (Interview, Johnson 2018)
46 (Interview, Mountcastle 2018)
47 Ibid.
48 (Interview, Johnson 2018)
49 (Interview, Maxson 2018)
50 Ibid.

References

Exponent Philanthropy. *History*. 2019. https://www.exponentphilanthropy.org/our-mission/history/ (accessed April 29, 2019).

Foundation Center. *Foundations*. 2019. http://data.foundationcenter.org/#/foundations/ (accessed April 29, 2019).

Johnson, Otis. Interview with David Maurrasse. Telephone Interview Recording. New York, April 5, 2018.

Maxson, Justin. Interview with David Maurrasse. Telephone Interview Recording. New York, April 3, 2018.

Mazyck, Bernie. Interview with Joey DeMarco. Telephone Interview Recording. New York, April 2, 2018.

Mountcastle, Laura. Interview with David Maurrasse. Telephone Interview Recording. New York, April 4, 2018.

7

INDIGENOUS AFRICAN PHILANTHROPY

TrustAfrica

Background on the Foundation

Simply put, philanthropy is the love for humanity. It is not peculiar to certain cultures of regions of the world: it exists in all societies. In that sense, philanthropy is universal. However, African philanthropy differs from traditional forms of Western philanthropy in both nature and the expressions it takes. Philanthropic activity in Africa is often masked by Western conceptions of "philanthropy".[1] There is an informality to African philanthropy, which is embedded in daily life, whereas Western philanthropy[2] tends to flow from structured, and often institutionalized, giving. Furthermore, Western philanthropy is often associated with giving by high net worth individuals; the basis of African philanthropy typically is among those of lower socioeconomic status.[3] This is not to suggest that philanthropic giving is not prevalent among those of modest financial means in Western nations. However, the dominant notion of Western philanthropy focuses on the wealthy. Actually, giving by high net worth individuals in Africa partaking in philanthropy is rather sensitive.[4] How gifts are recognized due to potential tax implications and questions regarding source of funds are among tensions surrounding giving by the wealthy in Africa. These issues can lead to underreporting of the quantity and type of philanthropy documented.[5]

The African Grantmakers Network identified six distinct trends emerging in African philanthropy[6]:

1. The continuation of informal models of giving across much of the continent – there is a clear preference for more direct channels of giving.
2. There is a lack of economic incentive and clear policy to promote strategic giving.

3. Very few linkages exist between different fields of giving, much of the philanthropy occurring is siloed in distinct buckets.
4. Tracking and evaluation of philanthropy is limited.
5. Much of the giving that occurs in Africa is through African donors – the presence of non-African donors is small.
6. The new generation of high net worth Africans prefer to merge philanthropy and business.

These trends provide a general picture of the nature and style of African philanthropy which, of course, varies from one nation to the next across a vast continent. Informality, for example, remains a preference as a pathway to "direct" giving. In this instance, one gives directly to a person or persons rather than through an incorporated organization. In the United States and some parts of Europe, philanthropy has become institutionalized. A growing nonprofit sector in the West is characterized by established officially incorporated organizations. Most foundations only contribute to incorporated organizations. Additionally, in many Western nations, a policy landscape is established to both provide incentives and regulate the nonprofit sector and the philanthropy that supports it.

Indeed, Western philanthropy has its own characteristics, which are not universal. Therefore, one should not assume that Western-style giving is the only manifestation of philanthropy. Concurrently, it is important to recognize the larger sums of money designated for philanthropic purposes in the West. The presence of these substantial assets is a reflection of historical distributions of accumulated wealth across the world – the historical economic disparities between the global North and South. It also reflects a history of intentional efforts to build and grow a nonprofit sector in certain Western nations. These factors influenced dynamics in the international grantmaking of Western foundations. Some Western foundations, such as the Ford Foundation have developed agendas for giving in developing countries including many nations within Africa.

Governments of African nations and African nongovernmental organizations have secured resources from Western foundations that have prioritized global giving. The presence of Western foundations in Africa brings another dynamic into our understanding of philanthropy in Africa. As noted, African philanthropy has already existed for generations. It is manifested differently than what is generally viewed as philanthropy in the United States and some parts of Europe or Canada. However, there is growth in African-based Western-style philanthropy. For example, over 130 philanthropic organizations have been established across the African continent. Philanthropy that is indigenous to Africa and Western foundations giving in Africa have been coexisting. But in the case of external foundations that contribute to African organizations, the same questions addressed in these pages apply – Who decides? How can intended beneficiary communities influence philanthropic giving? How can foundations incorporate the perspectives of grantees and grantee constituent communities into their giving priorities?

These questions confronted the Ford Foundation and African partners, which led to the creation of TrustAfrica.

The Ford Foundation was established in 1936 with an initial gift of US$25,000 by Edsel Ford, who was the son of the founder of the Ford Motor Company, Henry Ford. Now the Ford Foundation has a $12 billion endowment, and contributes $500 million in grants each year across the world.[7] The Ford Foundation makes investments in East Africa, West Africa, Southern Africa, and North Africa/the Middle East. The foundation's philosophy on giving has evolved over the years. A 2017 blog post by Kathy Reich, Director, Building Institutions and Networks (BUILD) at the Ford Foundation indicates various ways in which the practices of foundations can better contribute to change in the world. She identifies five areas of emphasis, the first of which is "empower", which she describes as follows: "Funders can consciously work to shift power dynamics with the organizations they support, emphasizing trust and partnership."[8] This is the kind of thinking that led to the creation of TrustAfrica.

TrustAfrica started as the Special Initiative for Africa (SIA)[9] at the Ford Foundation headquarters in New York. This initiative was developed in response to the May 2000 issue of *The Economist*, which presented Africa as a "Hopeless Continent". Subsequently, discussions of SIA began in 2001 after the Ford Foundation received a surge in the growth of its endowment. Between 2002 and 2005, SIA made numerous $200,000 grants to test the idea of grantmaking in Africa and to gauge the success of African Philanthropy. SIA was formally launched in Dakar, Senegal in 2006 and renamed TrustAfrica. TrustAfrica was founded based on a location agreement with Senegal's government and with a $30 million commitment from the Ford Foundation and an additional $600,000 in grant money to promote religious pluralism in Africa. During the last decade, TrustAfrica has experienced substantial growth in terms of its size and diversity of grants received, staff size and board composition; its assets now total $14 million. TrustAfrica is now celebrating 13 years as an independent foundation and manages various donor funds.

While the SIA was developed as an initiative of the Ford Foundation, TrustAfrica was conceptualized as and evolved into an independent organization, which is led by and serving Africans across the continent. TrustAfrica is governed by a Board of Directors, including eight members – five Trustees, the Executive Director, Treasurer and Chair. Board members hail from various African countries and are responsible for raising funds, building partnerships and serving as ambassadors for TrustAfrica. This leadership structure places Africans in a governing capacity and is intentionally representative of a range of African nations. The role of these Board members includes raising funds. Therefore, continued investment from the Ford Foundation is not only to provide a base of resources supporting the organization. It is intended to help catalyze TrustAfrica's ability to build a larger base of resources for philanthropic purposes in the continent.

TrustAfrica's mission is "to strengthen African initiatives that address the most difficult challenges confronting the continent".[10] It is this resolve and commitment to African issues that characterizes TrustAfrica as an indigenous foundation. Indigenous foundations are created in order to develop strategies that reflect the perspectives and interests of communities in a specific area and raise capital in order to meet a given community's needs. These are organizations that are by and for the intended beneficiary communities, placing decision making directly in the hands of these populations. As these foundations are representative of the populations they intend to serve, they are designed to be accountable to these constituencies. TrustAfrica's model of including Board members representative of the continent and raising money from those varying constituents is a structured attempt to ask populations to invest in philanthropy for their own communities.

The idea of an indigenous foundation can apply to any particular population. The distinction is a form of philanthropy representative of and governed by the population served. In this case, TrustAfrica is a foundation that is committed to address the challenges for the whole continent of Africa rather than a single country or locality or specific ethnic or identity group. This is a broad agenda. However, it is an approach that is in direct response to external philanthropy that does not listen to the population served – that gives *to* rather than *with* communities. In addition to serving a vast geographical area with substantial diversity within its target population, TrustAfrica has developed a comprehensive programmatic agenda. TrustAfrica's programs focus on three areas: securing the conditions for democracy; equitable development fostering African enterprise and achieving broadly shared prosperity; and cultivating African resources for democracy and development.[11] These programs provide services to impoverished communities. These are initiatives designed to alter the ways of life in African nations – changing how populations can engage democratically, and thus influence how leaders are chosen and how leadership is manifested. They help enhance the capacity of populations to build capital and sustain themselves collectively. Their agenda explicitly includes the cultivation of resources as well. The programming supports both development in the traditional sense of building capacity and growing capital, but also democracy in order to address broader concerns about how nations are governed and the inclusion of populations in governance. Transcending these two significant endeavors is the idea of continuing to build a base of African resources designed to support these two significant goals regarding democracy and development.

TrustAfrica fulfills its mission through collaboration with institutions and donors that share similar values. However, indigenous foundations in Africa might clash on ideals and visions with overseas donors given the aforementioned distinctions between Western and African philanthropy. In Africa, communities are philanthropic in their daily existence.[12] But, Western organized philanthropy is a different concept.[13] Consequently, indigenous foundations might favor local donors whose values align with the foundations' values.

TrustAfrica, while structured as an indigenous foundation, was created by Africans, some of whom had worked with the Ford Foundation in the U.S. and in Africa. Indeed, the values of the Ford Foundation and TrustAfrica are aligned. TrustAfrica was founded with a view to promoting African agency and amplifying African voices within the international donor community, and to allow the foundation and organizations to collaborate on projects not traditionally funded in their niches. New ideas and initiatives are also raised and tested at TrustAfrica, which mainly operates as a catalyst and convener. In addition, good governance and successful experiences are also shared and promoted by TrustAfrica among its grantees. TrustAfrica believes that its grantmaking strategies promote diversity; it strives to fund the forgotten organizations and to date, has helped establish entrepreneurial universities and improve agriculture.[14]

Indigenous foundations in general tend to make grants to organizations that are homegrown, smaller in size, and often overlooked by larger grantmaking organizations.[15] These grantee organizations are, more often than not, focused on particular issues on limited budgets due to low cash flow. However, these organizations are also ones that best understand the needs of local communities and have fostered a working relationship that positions them to create change and solve problems in their communities. In accordance with its mission and strategic approach, TrustAfrica has defined its core values as: collaboration among African institutions and formation of long-term relationships with grantees; maintaining the highest standards of institutional performance, which includes sound management, accountable and transparent governance, effective communication, and sustainable results; and forging closer ties with the African diaspora to strengthen global alliances for Africa.[16] The emphasis on smaller, perhaps more grassroots, organizations is compelling. This is another area of distinction with many Western foundations, which tend to support organizations with greater pre-existing organizational and financial capacity, on the assumption that these entities are best suited to achieve desired programming results. TrustAfrica and other indigenous foundations stress the degree of authentic connection between organizations and the communities they serve. These foundations invest in organizations that might not be noticed at all by more established foundations even if they are more reflective of their constituents.

TrustAfrica is not what would be considered a large foundation. According to TrustAfrica's annual report,[17] in 2017–2018 TrustAfrica held over $17.7 million in assets, with annual grants totaling $1.57 million. From 2006 to 2016, TrustAfrica has made 552 grants worth $27 million – 99% of them to organizations in African countries, particularly those in western, eastern and southern Africa. It is still in the beginnings of trying to build up trust and grantmaking in the Delta region of Nigeria. Currently, TrustAfrica does not have an endowment as there is conflict between utilizing money now, when there is great need, and building an endowment.[18] As Aidoo mentioned, "One has to be very careful about investments and endowments. Some investments can go against the mission of the foundation, against the values of the foundation."[19] While TrustAfrica struggles with traditional forms of endowment, it is instead looking towards individuals who are sentimentally attached to the foundation and willing to donate money to build an endowment.[20] In the meantime, the Ford Foundation provided $3 million per year to TrustAfrica during the first ten years of its existence, and continues to provide program support.

TrustAfrica's thinking regarding endowments represents another important distinction with many Western foundations. While there are some U.S.-based foundations, which have also chosen to spend down their assets (e.g. Atlantic Philanthropies, the Open Society Institute), the dominant model remains focused on endowment building. The idea is that endowed foundations can continue to grow and spend a small percentage of their assets on expenses and grants each year. This approach leads to organizations, like the Ford Foundation, which can exist in perpetuity and become continuous sources of support for nonprofits and communities. TrustAfrica maintains that the resources are needed now.

It is also interesting that the Ford Foundation remains a significant donor to TrustAfrica. Consequently, TrustAfrica has both created an indigenous foundation for Africa and harnessed Western philanthropy in order to fulfill this goal. This pathway takes advantage of the larger base of capital existing at a foundation such as Ford, while maintaining TrustAfrica's indigenous philosophy as a foundation by and for the continent. This model works when values are aligned. Given the Ford Foundation's emphasis on the empowerment of the constituent populations where it invests, it does not use its ongoing grants to TrustAfrica as a source of control. By design, TrustAfrica continues to be governed by Africans rather than Western donors.

Considerations for Particular Types of Foundation

Under international law, there is actually no official definition of the word "indigenous". However, the United Nations generally recognizes indigenous populations as self-sustaining and self-governing societies that have been marginalized and discriminated against due to the arrival of a settler population.[21] Throughout the years, indigenous people have often been the receivers of philanthropy, particularly in developing countries; this is especially the case for Africa. TrustAfrica is an example of a foundation emphasizing homegrown philanthropy. Foundations with a similar orientation present a different philanthropic paradigm, which can enable grantees greater flexibility. While this is a benefit that many indigenous foundations provide, many grantees in these locations are not accustomed to being asked what they truly want.[22] However, once this obstacle is navigated, these grantees and the communities they serve recognize the advantages of philanthropy that is customized to their needs.

The long-term success of indigenous foundations rests on their capacity to build up funds and remain independent. Many indigenous foundations are often reliant on external funders; unfortunately, this means that these foundations must report back to and follow the agenda of external funders. Founding Chair Gerry Salole calls this external "baggage".[23] Originally from the Ford Foundation, Salole became the first Board chair upon the founding of TrustAfrica. He currently serves on the Board, but as an honorary member. In his experience, many external funders often do not understand the full extent to how things are done in different countries. Foundations such as the Ford Foundation or Bill and Melinda Gates Foundation are based in the United States, while making grants in numerous other countries. While their staff can readily access the demographics of particular populations and investigate challenges facing these populations, these foundations lack the lived experiences of indigenous populations. These limitations can influence grantmaking. Some foundations hire staff to represent these populations who can provide better local context; but even in these instances, some important details can be overlooked. Local history, politics, culture, and customs are ubiquitous in the existence of anyone based in their home country. If one lives outside of this country, especially without having lived in the said country, it is very difficult to fully understand it. This reality can be true with respect to particular identity groups as well. Indigenous foundations essentially try to cut out the "middle-man" by having staff with lived experiences, who can directly translate to inform grantmaking strategies.[24]

The philosophy behind an indigenous foundation is very representative. But when the populations served by these foundations have limited financial resources, the process of garnering an adequate pool of funding can be quite arduous. As indigenous foundations highlight the significance of raising funds from local sources, they can struggle to identify willing contributors. Salole noted that "having good relationships to outside funders made it more complicated to raise money on the ground".[25] Furthermore, many indigenous foundations find themselves understaffed – a trade-off between ensuring most of their funds go towards grantees and still having enough staff to function organizationally. Salole highlighted two important challenges facing TrustAfrica. First of all, the hybrid nature of the foundation – concurrently leveraging the Ford Foundation's resources and aiming to raise money locally as an indigenous foundation – brings unique challenges in local resource development. Why should someone give to TrustAfrica if they have significant support from the Ford Foundation? Clearly, TrustAfrica has been able to overcome this perception to a degree. But many who are aware of the existence and role of larger donors may wonder why their funds matter in comparison to the much more substantial giving capacity of a foundation such as Ford. The idea of giving to TrustAfrica is about much more than raw finances. It is about a collective commitment to a philanthropic initiative that is by and for Africa.

Secondly, TrustAfrica's own philosophy emphasizes that money for the community organizations first and foremost can conflict with organizational capacity needs. While many larger foundations with endowments might operate out of immaculate facilities and provide significant salaries and benefits to staff, an indigenous foundation such as TrustAfrica remains a lean operation. Considerable resources spent on staffing and administration might even be a hindrance to raising money from local constituents. The image of TrustAfrica likely must prioritize spending for the community over the organization. However, the organization must be able to function effectively, and staff must survive. An indigenous foundation must continually strive to strike a proper balance in this regard.

Ese Emerhi, who has spent the last 18 years working in the international development field supporting human rights and is now the Project Director of Kiisi Trust Fund, a fund managed by TrustAfrica, said, "Philanthropy still feels like a foreign concept – we are using a Western term to describe this reality. Your average African is doing 'philanthropy' on a daily basis, naturally, without putting a name on it: you're paying for your cousin's school feels, you're paying for your cousin's house, etc. They are helping their neighbors and advancing their societies in one way or another but we don't call it philanthropy. It's just the 'African burden', it's your responsibility, it's how you grow up."[26] This short-term charity action is already ingrained in the people of Africa, but it is less systematic than traditional Western philanthropy and lacks formal structure and a longer-term view. Emerhi wonders if another term is necessary to describe indigenous philanthropy, something between charity and philanthropy, as the two terms do not quite fit. It seems that TrustAfrica combines elements of Africans supporting their own and philanthropy with long-range strategic goals. Some of the aspects of philanthropy Emerhi describes are a matter of survival. Some of the goals of TrustAfrica are transformative – changing the landscape of democracy and development. Local communities work toward these larger goals, but they could benefit from additional capital. This is where TrustAfrica can intervene.

Strategy – The Essence of the Foundation's Strategy

TrustAfrica funds across the entire continent of Africa. However, almost half of its grants are made for Western African countries followed by Southern and Eastern Africa; Central and Northern Africa are areas in which TrustAfrica hopes to increase grantmaking. Each year, the foundation makes around 30–60 grants.[27] TrustAfrica does not accept unsolicited proposals in order to break away from traditional forms of donor-advised philanthropy.[28]

Currently the strategy of TrustAfrica is to focus on African philanthropy by leveraging new and traditional forms of African giving to advance democracy and development. TrustAfrica builds upon existing African traditions of giving and sharing. A significant aspect of this strategy's intention is minimalizing the reliance on external donors. Janet Mawiyoo, TrustAfrica's Board member (and now Treasurer) is proud of the effort put into monitoring the process and impact of grants, "If you receive a grant, years down the road, TrustAfrica still cares and keeps in contact. Not all funding organizations are this diligent." TrustAfrica sees the organizations it funds as "partners," not "grantees," to help create a more collaborative relationship.

For Emerhi at the Kiisi Trust, a proactive "boots-on-the-ground" model is utilized to make grants. The staff are deliberate in incorporating community participation in its grantmaking process and Kiisi Trust's strategy is focused on identifying organizations that have never received funding.[29] Kiisi Trust has a separate Advisory Council that is predominantly composed of local stakeholders, community members and experts. The Council facilitates the grantmaking strategy by recommending "certain organizations and [Emerhi] reaches out to them. Typically, the Trustees approve the proposals reviewed by the Advisory Council. Then the organizations work on their official memorandum of understanding with TrustAfrica, which then cuts the check."[30] She lamented while this is a good strategy, it is a long process, lasting about five months. Many indigenous foundations, TrustAfrica included, struggle with solidifying a grantmaking strategy as these foundations are just getting started in the philanthropy world.

Community engagement is built into TrustAfrica's grantmaking approach. Staff are spending time in the communities in which the foundation makes investments. Grantees, as is the case with other foundations that prioritize inclusion of constituents in influencing program strategies, are viewed by TrustAfrica as "partners". Overall, the foundation's strategy drives toward goals around democracy and development, utilizing the mobilization of indigenous funds toward these ends. The implementation of this strategy is structurally inclusive, leveraging local perspectives to identify the kinds of organizations that are representing their communities and poised to address important concerns.

Commitment to Equity and Inclusion – The Foundation's Overall Commitment to Inclusion

For TrustAfrica, two components define its commitment to equity and inclusion. The first, raising money from African sources, is a strategic choice that helps fuel its commitment to equity and inclusion. Raising funds from African sources guarantees that external agendas are not at the forefront of grantmaking strategies, and the organizations and programs being funded are truly what is needed for the community. However, as Emerhi mentioned, sometimes external funding is more easily acquired than internal funding. But in these instances, the agendas of external funders must also be considered, which may decrease opportunities to further equity and inclusion. With this possibility in mind, TrustAfrica incorporated a safeguard for these two principles into its grantmaking strategy. TrustAfrica does not just focus on the issues of one village of a particular country; it funds organizations all over the African continent.[31] This ensures that all organizations are given an equal chance to promote their work with grant money. Trust Africa believes its broad approach not only encompasses more areas and people, but expands TrustAfrica's diversity and inclusivity.[32]

One obstacle that stands in the way of TrustAfrica's commitment to inclusion is that in many parts of Africa, especially in South Africa, a large portion of the wealth belongs to white individuals, making it difficult to take that wealth and disperse it among other communities. However, in terms of TrustAfrica's internal commitment to inclusion, the foundation gives grantees a lot of freedom in defining their project activities. According to Emerhi, "TrustAfrica has worked with more than 500 grantee partners, and has a wide footprint across the continent, more than any other philanthropic organization in Africa."[33] TrustAfrica's staff, she said, are "intentional about finding those hidden voices and those foundations that are not celebrated."[34] For instance, Kiisi Trust is focusing on organizations that work on marginalized spaces. One of their partners currently works with homeless kids while another partner works on changing the demographic structure of the Ogoni people to allow Ogoni women to have bigger voices in their community and in their domestic lives. One interesting aspect of this indigenous foundation is that larger, more well-established organizations often do not even apply for TrustAfrica grants, opening the way for smaller organizations to receive funding.

TrustAfrica has begun to establish itself as a foundation that is by and for the African continent. It has become known for supporting organizations that are representative of their communities and not already plugged into larger-scale institutional philanthropy. They are quite cognizant of the degree of control that can come from philanthropic giving. They are aware of the potential influences of sources of funding, and have had to confront challenging issues such as race among South African donors.

Manifestations of Commitment — Techniques and Practices

How Inclusion Informs Strategy Programmatically

Programmatically, Emerhi notes that "TrustAfrica is not just about giving out grants but also accompanying the grantees through capacity building. We also provide capacity to teach how to read and learn how to do a budget. We are flexible with the format. Some of these organizations are so rural, they may not even have an office. There is a lot of capacity building that comes with that. It's a proactive grantmaking model."[35] She then goes on to discuss: "With Kiisi, we are working with local community service organizations (CSOs) on the ground, some of them have never received funding from an external source before. We do very small grants (less than $5,000) and we call it 'acupuncture grants'. We focus on small amounts to allow small organizations to grow."[36]

The reality of this approach is that it is more time-consuming. It takes both staff time and effort to visit each CSO, vet the organization, initiate communication about grant objectives and follow-up with organizations following the grant period. As Emerhi indicated, she can "spend a whole week working on a budget with a grantee". However, the patience and time put in by staff at TrustAfrica has paid off according to Victor Ochen from Golden Tulip, a grantee organization. He has nothing but praise for TrustAfrica. Ochen was born and raised in Uganda during the war and through his lived experience was inspired to build a peace-building effort in Africa. He has "gotten millions of dollars from different organizations but I never experienced the dignity, respect and trust that I had with TrustAfrica – not even with the United Nations or any of the other funders I had."[37] As previously noted, indigenous philanthropy seeks to work directly with individuals with lived experiences and local communities to foster trust and create change.

One great challenge to philanthropy that is accountable and connected to the communities that stand to benefit the most from giving, is the capacity of partner organizations (often known as "grantees"). The commitment of TrustAfrica to the communities it serves means additional time, attention, and resources toward strengthening partner organizations. Yet this is the type of investment that is required in order to improve these communities. TrustAfrica is pursuing necessary work given its intentions. Ochen's perspective, as a TrustAfrica partner, speaks to another important dimension of TrustAfrica's programmatic approach. The foundation's relationships to partners are fundamentally stressing trust and respect. How foundations enter communities and engage constituents is a crucial component in the execution of philanthropic agendas. In the case of TrustAfrica, the processes of community engagement and collaboration with partner organizations is a reflection of the foundation's values.

How Inclusion Informs Strategy Institutionally

A commitment to inclusion is reflected in TrustAfrica's institutional composition and structure. The staff at TrustAfrica truly understand the challenges that are on the ground. All of their staff possess lived experiences in Africa. Many speak several native languages, and most have, at some point in their lives, worked with community based organizations or NGOs either connected to or based in Africa. Structurally, TrustAfrica maintains a very limited overhead so that 80 percent of its money can go directly to grantees. One way that TrustAfrica keeps overhead low is by working virtually with its grantees and using an online grant management system. Kiisi Trust's $5 million endowment was the result of an out-of-court settlement by Shell. Here again, TrustAfrica is leveraging funds from an external source in order to address local priorities. Also notice that TrustAfrica's structure allows for endowed funds to exist within the broader organization. Here TrustAfrica harnesses aspects of a community foundation's design to develop different pots of resources carrying specific intentions.

Much of the funding for TrustAfrica continues to come from the Ford Foundation. As Salole knows, grant making is "not a money-making business, it will always depend on some donors, but there are many examples of privatized foundations [through] selling of an industry the government doesn't know how to run [or] an oil company that needs to make reparation to a specific area because of the damage it's done...TrustAfrica could be a good vehicle for that type of assets."[38] This has been discussed with the eight TrustAfrica Board members that meet twice a year. On a separate note, Salole mentions that TrustAfrica's Board is diverse when it comes to gender, country of origin, historical background and religion. Current board members hail from Ethiopia, South Africa, Zimbabwe, Kenya, Gambia, and Mali, and have held a variety of human justice or advocacy positions in the United Nations or nonprofits around the world before settling at TrustAfrica.[39]

While TrustAfrica emphasizes indigenous resources, it is very open to securing resources from external sources, and using those funds to advance the foundation's mission. TrustAfrica is designed to be by and for Africa in its giving, community engagement, governance, and staffing. The commitment to inclusion of African voices pervades all aspects of the organization. However, they recognize where most resources reside. These financial resources are not plentiful in the communities in which TrustAfrica invests. In order for TrustAfrica to embody its mission, it must secure financial buy-in from indigenous donors. This journey toward local resource development continues. Concurrently, the Ford Foundation remains an important partner that enables TrustAfrica to continue to grow and advance.

Progress – What Has Been the Impact of these Approaches? How Do They Measure Progress?

While TrustAfrica is designed to invest across the continent, there are only so many areas in which the foundation could have had a meaningful impact since its foundation. This is still a relatively young organization. One area in which TrustAfrica is a new player is the Niger Delta. It has worked extensively with other regions in Africa, but are just beginning to make grants in the Delta area. Less than one percent of their funding has gone to the Delta region in the past ten years.[40] In this region, trust has been difficult to build. But in the areas that TrustAfrica has an established presence and a record of doing good work, the name TrustAfrica is trusted.

For Emerhi, this is because "[The communities] know TrustAfrica, they are comfortable with it, [and] they understand the model and the goal of advancing philanthropy in Africa. For now, the inclusive approach of the Kiisi Trust is to increase the visibility of TrustAfrica in the Niger Delta. TrustAfrica has struggled to keep countries in Africa informed of their work. It is difficult as the Delta region of Africa is more isolated. With time, this is something that can they can overcome, Emerhi believes, "We just have to keep pushing. Keep asking the question: what can we do in Tunisia, what should we be doing? If you want to do things carefully, you may want to force yourself to think outside the box." To date, Kiisi Trust has distributed $337,600 to Northern Africa and the Delta region.[41]

Overall, TrustAfrica has developed a presence in numerous segments of a very extensive and diverse continent. The desire to continue to cover as many regions as possible is evident in its interest in deepening communication and trust in the Delta region. Given its resources, TrustAfrica's mission is quite ambitious. It appears that the organization has already helped change mindsets about philanthropy and its potential. The organization has gotten numerous grants to organizations that otherwise would not have received funding, and helped build the capacity of these organizations to become more effective over time.

Learning – What Has the Foundation Learned from Their Approaches? How Have They Used Learning to Inform Institutional and Programmatic Change?

With all that it has learned, TrustAfrica continues to be a pioneer for African philanthropy. It has published many reports on African philanthropy. In 2011, it published a book in conjunction with Southern Africa Trust[42] about the legislative environment for civil society in 18 countries in Central, East and Southern Africa. It continues to publish annual reports to describe operations and financial conditions, research reports, policy briefs and articles on what it has learned about making philanthropy work in Africa on its website. Much of what has been learned focuses on the types of legislative modifications that are needed to encourage African philanthropy. Salole hopes that TrustAfrica will inspire other foundations, and "have people take much more seriously the idea of an institution that can handle the re-grant resources with integrity, with a flair".

One example of an institution that has tried to emulate TrustAfrica is the Southern African Trust. It was established in 2005 to support civil society organizations in Southern Africa so that voices of the poor have a larger and better impact on the development of public policies. Similar to TrustAfrica, the Southern African Trust provides funding to organizations that are dedicated to the reduction of poverty and inequality and work to improve human rights, economic development and capacity training[43]. Furthermore, the Southern African Trust has adopted TrustAfrica's ideals of quality grantmaking, regardless of organization size. Salole believes that "TrustAfrica has been successful from the point of view of creating an entity that is closer to the ground and can respond more appropriately to an issue, especially if you are working in conflict areas. You couldn't have done if you weren't an African foundation, you wouldn't get the same access. They were able to choose people on the ground. It wasn't a ready-made recipe, looking from a blue print. They were able to adjust and observe. They took the time to do that."[44]

One thing that TrustAfrica hopes to strive for going forward is more diverse representation among African nations on their Board. As of now, there is often repetition in nationality as retiring board members bring in new members of the same nationality. TrustAfrica has also realized the difficulty in achieving a full partnership with grantees. It has identified many of the obstacles that exist in realizing this goal. Akwasi Aidoo, is the former Executive Director of TrustAfrica. He possesses extensive experience in African philanthropy and prior to TrustAfrica, headed the Ford Foundation's offices in Senegal and Nigeria. He became the Executive Director of TrustAfrica because of his experience in Africa and work at the Ford Foundation. He discussed these difficulties, "It's very easy for people to have the intention and not really sustain it. On our part, it was also hard to sustain it because it was a lot of work, the money had to go out quickly, and we have a lot of grantees. We make quite a lot of progress, I'd say 50%. It's an area where foundations as a whole need to pay more attention. And then the final thing is the notion and somehow, a partnership would imply a level playing field. It's a good idea but the determinants are not always in your hands. Each one of [the foundations] come to the table with their own agenda, and we are an intermedium."

TrustAfrica has been influential in its relatively short existence. But it has also learned about the challenges of being a representative foundation for a large continent, the need for resources that can sustain this broad purpose, and the execution of distributing multiple grants to organizations dispersed in various communities. TrustAfrica constructed a vehicle for African philanthropy that did not exist. Moreover, the foundation altered thinking about African philanthropy, as in the case of the Southern African Trust's adoption of TrustAfrica's approach.

Direction – What Are the Foundation's Future Intentions?

Between October 2006 and March 2016, TrustAfrica distributed a total of 552 grants that total more than $27,048,152.[45] While the majority of its funding has gone to Western Africa, it has also funded numerous projects in Eastern and Southern Africa. Central Africa followed by Northern Africa received the lowest amount of funding. On a continental level, TrustAfrica helped establish the Centre for Citizens Participation at the African Union and the African Philanthropy Network in order to develop a community of practice and strengthen the growing field.[46]

In the past eight years, TrustAfrica has built itself up from an idea from the Ford Foundation to its own independent foundation run on the ideals of African philanthropy. Its concept has inspired the formation of several other foundations in Africa also dedicated to tapping into the roots of African philanthropy. TrustAfrica has published numerous reports and findings to help educate and inspire others in Africa to engage in philanthropy for the betterment of all. Now, as they move into another year as an independent foundation, developing and maintaining an endowment is of high importance to them, as is continuing to fund grassroots organizations. While the idea of an endowment holds some resources back from communities, it can sustain a philanthropic organization such as TrustAfrica.

As with all foundations and organizations, there are countless things that can be improved and continually addressed. For Salole, there is not one specific thing that is missing, but one thing that Salole points out is that TrustAfrica does not work in the early childhood field, because it is too small to do everything. TrustAfrica does not have the tools necessary to support organizations in this field. TrustAfrica funds three program areas – political justice, socioeconomic justice, and philanthropy and advisory services.[47] These three program areas were selected because of their ability to impart deep positive impacts to African society. In 2017, TrustAfrica distributed grants to organizations in Nigeria, South African and Tanzania to further socioeconomic rights, economic justice and improve agricultural development.[48] However, this is not to say that future grants cannot focus on improving early childhood. In the meantime, TrustAfrica plans to continue to make a level playing field, develop organic relationships and increase the number of African funding partners. Aidoo suggested a potential idea:

"One way to make this work is through a network of African foundations for our grantees. So, we engineered the setting up of the African Philanthropic Network. We thought we could get some of the major African airlines to have in-flight giving programs where the small change people have when they travel, they deposit it to the cabin crew. The change donations would then be used for specific countries and places, and for something that is critical for those countries. Such an idea would make institutions like TrustAfrica and the others very authentic and organic."

TrustAfrica is still a blossoming foundation. Its youth allows it to more easily modify grantmaking strategies and relationships with grantees. With ten years of experience under its belt, it can now begin to solidify a strategic plan that continues to incorporate in its commitment to African issues, equity and authenticity.

Conclusions and Lessons Learned (Including Implications for the Particular Type of Foundation that TrustAfrica Is)

Indigenous foundations like TrustAfrica carry numerous benefits – they are local, known and trusted within a community and are able to fund areas that are often overlooked by other Foundations but undeniably important. As evident in the case of TrustAfrica, these types of foundations have difficulty securing adequate funding from local sources. Most often, funding comes from external sources, whose goals and values do not always align. There is a continued need to encourage the investment of local communities and funds. The hallmark of Indigenous foundations is to work closely with grantee organizations and to listen to their desires and needs. However, this is time consuming and does not always manifest due to staffing and financial constraints.

Western-style philanthropy is still just emerging in Africa. Therefore, TrustAfrica's framework and strategy are significant innovations. The foundation needs the flexibility when it comes to both fundraising and allocating funds, as its limited funds can hamper its ability to partner with organizations across all of Africa.

This flexibility will allow TrustAfrica to continue to grow its network, quickly adapt to what is needed and grow its roots into the community.

Beyond financial resources and organizational capacity, TrustAfrica is positioned to alter the mindset of philanthropy focused on Africa and various developing countries. TrustAfrica is presenting a paradigmatic shift in thinking about funders and recipients of funding. Lessons from TrustAfrica's approach to listening to local community-based organizations with limited funding, for example, bring new insights into grantmaking strategies and decisions. While some foundations in the U.S. and Europe may have begun to engage grantees more directly and pursue strategies such as participatory grantmaking, there is something different about applying these approaches within nations and cultural contexts that have entirely different conceptions of philanthropy. Additionally, many African nations do not possess the level of financial resources required to address substantial social, political, and economic needs for historically impoverished populations.

A history of colonialism has shaped dynamics that are reflected in the relationship between Western foundations and developing countries. This is demonstrated in a mindset that foundations have resources and knowledge and local communities in developing countries do not. The approach of a foundation such as TrustAfrica changes this mindset. It values community voices and finds value in community organizations that were overlooked and viewed as lacking the capacity to combat the challenges facing their own communities. The TrustAfrica approach suggests that African voices not only have knowledge, but have the most important knowledge based on lived experiences, to define philanthropic priorities. Indeed, larger external foundations that wield the most substantial philanthropic resources could learn from TrustAfrica's values and methods. While TrustAfrica could benefit tremendously from considerably more resources than they already possess, they have already taught lessons about philanthropy and society that can maximize the impact of philanthropic giving.

Notes

1 (African Grantmakers Network 2018)
2 Ibid.
3 Ibid.
4 Ibid.
5 Ibid.
6 Ibid.
7 (Ford Foundation, *About Ford – Our Origins*, 2019)
8 (Reich 2017)
9 (Trust Africa 2016)
10 (TrustAfrica, *About Us*, 2019)
11 (TrustAfrica, *Programme*, 2019)
12 (Interview, Emerhi 2018)
13 Ibid.
14 (TrustAfrica, *Grant Database*, 2019)
15 Ibid.

16 (TrustAfrica, *About Us*, 2019)
17 (TrustAfrica, *Annual Reports*, 2019)
18 (Interview, Aidoo 2018)
19 Ibid.
20 Ibid.
21 (University of British Columbia 2019)
22 (Interview, Emerhi 2018)
23 (Interview, Salole 2018)
24 (TrustAfrica, *About Us – Our Staff*, 2019)
25 (Interview, Salole 2018)
26 (Interview, Emerhi 2018)
27 (TrustAfrica, *Grants*, 2019)
28 (TrustAfrica, *Grants – Grantmaking Policy*, 2019)
29 (Interview, Emerhi 2018)
30 Ibid.
31 (Interview, Aidoo 2018)
32 (Interview, Emerhi 2018)
33 Ibid.
34 Ibid.
35 Ibid.
36 Ibid.
37 (Interview, Ochen 2018)
38 (Interview, Salole 2018)
39 (TrustAfrica, *About Us – Board*, 2019)
40 (TrustAfrica, *Grants*, 2019)
41 (TrustAfrica, *The Kiisi Trust to Benefit the Ogoni People*, 2019)
42 The Trust mandate is to work on a non-profit basis, to undertake activities that contribute to the reduction of poverty and inequality (https://www.southernafricatrust.org/).
43 (Southern Africa Trust, *About*, 2019)
44 (Interview, Salole 2018)
45 (TrustAfrica, *Grants*, 2019)
46 Ibid.
47 (TrustAfrica, *Programme – Philanthropy Advisory Services*, 2019)
48 (TrustAfrica, *Grant Database*, 2019)

References

Africa Philanthropy Network. *Frameworks for a New Narrative Of African Philanthropy*. 2018. https://africaphilanthropynetwork.org/2018/08/28/frameworks-for-a-new-narrative-of-african-philanthropy/ (accessed March 29, 2019).
Aidoo, Akwasi. Interview with David Maurrasse and Franck Gbaguidi. Personal Interview. February 16, 2018.
Emerhi, Ese. Interview with Franck Gbaguidi. Personal Interview. February 2, 2018.
Ford Foundation. *About Ford – Our Origins*. 2019. https://www.fordfoundation.org/about/about-ford/our-origins/ (accessed March 20, 2019).
Ochen, Victor. Interview with Franck Gbaguidi. Personal Interview. February 12, 2018.
Reich, Kathy. How changing funder practices can change the world. *Ford Foundation – Ideas*. 2017. https://www.fordfoundation.org/ideas/equals-change-blog/posts/how-changing-funder-practices-can-change-the-world/ (accessed March 20, 2019).
Salole, Gerry. Interview with Franck Gbaguidi. Personal Interview. February 12, 2018.

Southern Africa Trust. *About.* 2019. http://www.southernafricatrust.org/about-southern-africa-trust/ (accessed March 24, 2019).

TrustAfrica. *A Decade of Strengthening African Initiatives - Press Release.* 2016. http://www.trustafrica.org/en/resource/news/item/3263-a-decade-of-strengthening-african-initiatives-press-release (accessed March 21, 2019).

TrustAfrica. *About Us.* 2019. http://trustafrica.org/en/about-us (accessed March 22, 2019).

TrustAfrica. *About Us – Board.* 2019. http://www.trustafrica.org/en/about-us/board/item/3402-sibongile-mkhabela-trustee (accessed March 25, 2019).

TrustAfrica. *About Us – Our Staff.* 2019. http://www.trustafrica.org/en/about-us/our-staff (accessed March 23, 2019).

TrustAfrica. *Annual Reports.* 2019. http://trustafrica.org/en/publications-trust/annual-reports (accessed March 23, 2019).

TrustAfrica. *Grants.* 2019. http://www.trustafrica.org/en/grants/grants-at-glance (accessed March 25, 2019).

TrustAfrica. *Grant Database.* 2019. http://www.trustafrica.org/en/grants/grants-database/grant/511-ta-16-021 (accessed March 23, 2019).

TrustAfrica. *Grants – Grantmaking Policy.* 2019. http://www.trustafrica.org/en/grants/our-grantmaking-policy (accessed March 25, 2019).

TrustAfrica. *Programme.* 2019. http://www.trustafrica.org/en/programme (accessed March 22, 2019).

TrustAfrica. *Programme – Philanthropy Advisory Services.* 2019. http://trustafrica.org/en/programme/philanthropy-advisory-services (accessed March 24, 2019).

TrustAfrica. *The Kiisi Trust to Benefit the Ogoni People.* 2019. http://www.trustafrica.org/en/kiisi-trust-fund (accessed March 24, 2019).

University of British Columbia. *Indigenous Foundations.* 2019. https://indigenousfoundations.arts.ubc.ca/global_actions/ (accessed January 11, 2019).

8

LESSONS FROM PRACTICE

Inclusively Strategic

The foundations featured herein are of varying types and operating in very different locales. They represent a wide range of asset bases as well, from relatively small foundations to a multi-billion-dollar institution such as the Conrad Hilton Foundation. It is notable that there is much to learn about innovation in philanthropy from smaller foundations. Overall, these foundations were identified because they were willing to broaden their conception of how to shape their strategic direction. They are exploring ways to involve the populations they hope to impact in their programming in designing their philanthropic strategies. Therefore, these foundations are *inclusively strategic*.

The manner in which each of the profiled foundations includes external voices in strategic planning varies significantly, although there are some striking similarities among them. Some of them emphasize restructuring the composition of their institutions, ensuring that they more adequately represent the populations most impacted by their program priorities. Some more strongly stress external engagement in their approach. Overall, however, each of these foundations is in pursuit of some kind of holistic transformation of how they operate as institutions. They all acknowledge that they are on some form of a "journey" toward a different kind of institution, which departs from many traditional paradigms in philanthropy. Therefore, if these, and some other, foundations continue to move in a transformative direction, the field of philanthropy will start to change as well. This will have implications on how foundations consider designing their strategies.

Strategic philanthropy is often associated with focused programming tied to specific outcomes and indicators. The development of strategy, in many foundations, is often insular in which priorities are determined internally. Once strategic priorities are developed, foundations seek out grantees that fit their guidelines. The concept of strategic philanthropy emerged as a way to transcend scattered approaches to giving in which foundations or donors lack guidelines, and merely give to a wide array of organizations that request funding. The aggregate of grantees in these scenarios can amount to limited focus and minimal impact. Foundations were well-intentioned to move in the direction of strategic philanthropy in order to be more accountable to contributing to demonstrable change.

Simultaneously, over the last couple of decades, foundations have been questioned over their insularity and lack of representation. Calls for greater diversity, equity, and inclusion (DEI) in philanthropy have increased and become much more prominent. Challenges to foundations regarding DEI have come in many forms. Foundations have been challenged to become more diverse and inclusive in their hiring, grantmaking, executive leadership, Boards, purchasing, and investments. Some foundations, such as the California Endowment, have developed tools to comprehensively assess their progress in all of these areas and more through their Diversity, Equity, and Inclusion Audit.[1] Attention to the equitable distribution of resources in philanthropy has grown as well. The concept of equity in general has become an increasing point of emphasis, challenging foundations to pursue the removal of barriers to opportunity so that all populations can advance without issues such as race or gender determining life outcomes. Some foundations are focusing their entire strategic direction on equity, as is the case with the San Francisco Foundation and the Meyer Memorial Trust.

The experiences of the six profiled foundations represent the convergence of strategic philanthropy and DEI. In many ways, foundations were right to become more focused and prioritize results. But strategic philanthropic approaches that are not connected to the populations that stand the most to gain from improved education or health, or whichever pressing issues, are doomed to fail. They are devoid of reality. They could be infused with great intelligence, spreadsheets, and data points; but if they are not informed by the lived experiences of the populations most impacted, they cannot hope to understand the complexity of their lives. One cannot expect greater educational outcomes for low income African American children without a comprehensive understanding of the reality of this population's experiences. Greater inclusion of foundations' constituencies should lead to more effective foundations in the long run. It is clear that these six profiled foundations are trying to become better philanthropic institutions that are more relevant to the contemporary realities of the populations they intend to serve.

An Array of Approaches and Tactics

As these foundations are all inclusively strategic in their own way, they are employing myriad approaches and tactics in so doing. Once a foundation begins to broaden its thinking about how to be more responsive to constituents, numerous techniques emerge. Some of these foundations have been creative and courageous in altering their practices.

Community Engagement

These foundations are actively engaging their constituent communities. For the San Francisco Foundation, this means organizing Listening Sessions in which populations in various neighborhoods and regions share their perspectives on priority issues facing their communities. The foundation used the learning from these sessions to shape its strategic plan. Based on the feedback it received, the foundation decided to focus their overall programming on equity with an emphasis on people, power, and place.

For the Conrad Hilton Foundation, this means direct communication with constituents in Africa to inform their international programming. The LankellyChase Foundation is spending time and engaging constituents in various cities in the U.K. to understand the dynamics that lead to severe disadvantages before deciding on how the foundation will intervene to contribute to solving the problems identified. The Mary Reynolds Babcock Foundation is similarly visiting communities in states in the American South to engage and learn, and invest accordingly.

Changing Staff Roles

These foundations realize that to effectively change the nature of their work in order to be more responsive to community needs, the role of staff has to change. Program staff in particular, tend to operate within specific defined themes and make grants from a distance. To varying degrees, the profiled foundations have been grappling with how to design staffing around engagement. Lankelly Chase's program staff are Action Inquiry Managers rather than "Program Officers". Their role is to inquire in various communities and help support actions that can address the matters about which they have learned through dialogue. The Mary Reynolds Babcock Foundation has Network Officers who visit communities and work with networks of organizations working toward common goals. The San Francisco Foundation realized that its new approach based on broad themes was not conducive to its traditional staffing model based on defined program areas. Therefore, the foundation is working on getting staff to work beyond single issues.

Participatory Grantmaking

In some of these foundations, constituents are participating in how funding is distributed. When a foundation makes a contribution, typically, internal actors (staff and Board) decide. In the case of a foundation, such as Lankelly Chase, the ultimate decision might come from the foundation, but the entire process of determining what should be funded is co-created at the community level. Lankelly Chase does not even use the term, "grants". It seeks to identify the problems, understand how systems work, and communicate with local constituents about who should be involved in addressing issues and how. Subsequently, the foundation would invest in a group of entities to address the issue, and the foundation would continue to remain a partner. Its approach is more of a partnership model.

Networks

A greater understanding of the issues facing communities has led some of these foundations to find ways to transcend single issues in their funding. The Mary Reynolds Babcock Foundation supports networks. It supports groups of organizations working comprehensively on multiple intersecting issues in specific regions. Support for networks allows a foundation to work beyond silos, crossing organizational and issue boundaries. Lankelly Chase's approach also lends itself to engaging networks, as it seeks to understand systems in specific places, and how the various actors in ecosystems of people and organizations relate in a locality. This is not a single-issue approach; it is about systems. Ultimately, the foundation partners with networks of organizations in a system to enable comprehensive solutions to complex problems.

Long-Term Support

These foundations generally recognize that short-term grants will not solve the pressing issues facing communities that have been historically disadvantaged. Most of the profiled foundations have had to review their approach to grantmaking, and consider how to make longer term investments. The idea of foundations deciding to support networks in order to address complex issues lends itself to longer term grants. As so many foundations make grants for a single year, tied to highly specified outcomes, those foundations that are pursuing strategies to address issues comprehensively alongside networks of partners are leaning toward grants over no fewer than three years with broader anticipated outcomes.

Board Composition

Another important way to be inclusively strategic is to bring perspectives from the community on the Board. This approach places representative voices in an ultimate decision-making role. It brings the community into the institution. TrustAfrica is an example of a foundation that is by and for a constituent population. As so much of grantmaking for African development has tended to come from outside of the continent historically, the emergence of TrustAfrica was a way to alter this trend. Created by the Ford Foundation as a way to grow African philanthropy, TrustAfrica is an entirely African organization with Board members from various African nations. This approach brings indigenous insights into giving to African organizations and places decision making in the hands of Africans.

The Mary Reynolds Babcock Foundation's approach to engaging constituents and investing in networks of organizations in various Southern communities was informed by the foundation's Board. As a family foundation, it spent many years with a Board of family members. When the foundation decided to open up the process and recruit Board members with a deep understanding of the communities in which it invests, the foundation changed. The family members listened to the non-family Board members and changed their approach in order to be more responsive to the realities of Southern communities. Now it is investing in networks and leveraging funding from other sources, and making long-term commitments to communities that are leading to more impactful results.

Staff Composition

Staff composition is important in a few ways. As previously noted, staff roles must adapt to significant institutional change in policy and practice. In order to successfully change staff roles, it is also important to consider staff characteristics. Indeed, this is the case regarding competencies. Foundations that are more deeply engaged in communities and working across issues require staff with the competency to implement accordingly. But they also require staff with lived experiences that help the institution better understand the issues facing the communities they hope to help. They bring to the organization a deeply personal sense of lived experiences. The Meyer Memorial Trust has been very cognizant of the role of staff composition in shaping the foundation's work. In their "equity journey", the Trust was highly intentional about diversifying its staff and Board. Ultimately, it hired an African American woman CEO who brought an existing commitment to diversity, equity, and inclusion to the foundation in order to bring the foundation into another phase of its journey.

The Conrad Hilton Foundation, in its international programming in Africa, recognized that it would be best to hire African staff to manage this work and be the liaison between the foundation and African governments and other constitutions in the countries where the foundation has a presence. As TrustAfrica's Board represents African nations, its staff does as well. This is a part of the overall business model of this foundation that is intended to both represent and support African communities.

Internal Policies

All of the profiled foundations had to review their internal policies and practices to be consistent with their emerging values and intentions. In addition to composition, these foundations are reviewing how they make decisions, how they use their assets, how they evaluate, how they communicate, and other matters.

Common Themes

Pursuing Comprehensive Institutional Change

These foundations have in common an ambition toward comprehensively changing as institutions. They hope to build on their current approaches now that they have altered their thinking about their role in relationship to constituents and broader ideas about equity and inclusion. The LankellyChase Foundation, for example, hopes to further devolve decision making and become more of a partner to U.K. communities. TrustAfrica is far from where they hope to be, as it is a newer institution. It is attempting to be a home for African philanthropists to establish funds in addition to using its existing capital. The Meyer Memorial Trust is seeking to demonstrate their commitment to equity in every aspect of its foundation. The Conrad Hilton Foundation, as it continues to grow, is looking to become more reflective of the communities they hope to impact. None of these foundations are satisfied with the work they have done to date. They have greater ambitions, and hope to continue on some form of a "journey" toward a broader vision.

Recognizing the Significance of Place

Any foundation has only so much money or other resources. Focus is important for effectiveness. One way in which these foundations have focused their attention and investment has been in place. Equity issues are manifested in place. Certainly, a community foundation such as the San Francisco Foundation has an inherent emphasis on the locality where it is based. But within a broad region, it realized that, in order to engage communities in Listening Sessions, it had to identify and visit particular neighborhoods within the region. The Conrad Hilton Foundation selects particular areas in Africa for its investments and partnerships. The LankellyChase Foundation is involved in "inquiries" in particular cities within the broader U.K. region. The Mary Reynolds Babcock Foundation invests in networks in specific places in the South. The Meyer Memorial Trust is even more focused on particular places in the state of Oregon.

A place-based approach is fundamentally connected to being inclusively strategic. Strengthened lines of communication with constituents, in some ways, depend upon understanding lived experiences. These experiences are manifested in places. One's housing, employment, health care, air quality, and other issues are manifested in place. As foundation resources can extend only so far, it is also logical to channel philanthropic resources toward improving conditions in localities. Learning from these efforts in place can have universal value. Therefore, as these foundations hope to bring about greater equity in the communities they emphasize, they are making a contribution to equity in general.

Confronting Power Dynamics

The irony in philanthropy is that foundations have missions in order to improve the lives of disadvantaged communities. But they are extensions of the wealth that was created to facilitate inequities in society. Moreover, the dynamic between foundations and grantees represents a significant power dynamic that often creates tensions. Foundations also wield a great deal of flexibility in comparison to many institutions in other industries. Endowed foundations have an established financial security that is uncommon in many other settings. Therefore, we look to foundations, which are powerful institutions to dismantle inequities and empower the disenfranchised.

The foundations profiled in this book, to varying degrees are challenging power dynamics in philanthropy. Indeed, they are still foundations, thus continuing to wield a certain amount of power. But they are exploring how they can give up some of that power for a greater good. The very act of opening up communication about how foundation resources are invested to external constituents is a form of challenging a traditional power dynamic. A foundation such as Lankelly Chase is fairly explicit about confronting its own power as a philanthropic institution. TrustAfrica's very existence is a response to a particular type of power dynamic in which foundations external to a particular community wield disproportionate power over constituents they are supporting, as those constituents are dependent on outside funding. TrustAfrica is attempting to build philanthropic capital that is by and for Africans in order to limit this dependency. The Meyer Memorial Trust's commitment to an "equity journey" is a decision to continually confront the power dynamics inherent in philanthropy.

Breaking with Tradition

One aspect of challenging power dynamics in philanthropy is breaking with tradition. The foundations profiled herein have assessed various limitations to traditional foundation practices, and considered new approaches. From how grants are distributed to how programs are organized to how program officers operate; these foundations are not afraid to depart from tradition. If equity and inclusion are the goals, foundations must consider what they might have to do differently in order to be successful. The Mary Reynolds Babcock Foundation was not afraid to change when it decided to break with tradition and bring non-family members on the Board. The Meyer Memorial Trust has a built-in green light to continually innovate through its own charter from its founder. This is an interesting example of a situation where a founder explicitly did not want to hamper the foundation's ability to evolve and innovate. The LankellyChase Foundation was courageous enough to reflect and decide to refer to "grantees" as "partners" and alter its entire approach from "programs" to "inquiries".

Ultimately, these institutions are trying to become better foundations, and become as relevant as possible given the circumstances facing the communities they hope to improve. This may mean challenging norms, mindsets, and practices, and being willing to change.

Embracing Risk and Uncertainty

Similarly, these foundations have demonstrated a willingness to embrace risk as well as uncertainly. One interesting byproduct of the move toward strategic philanthropy among foundations is to find safer bets, which can provide measurable outcomes. This risk aversion often leads to disproportionate contributions to organizations with substantial financial and other forms of capacity. In this scenario, organizations that might be more grassroots and representative of lower income communities or communities of color or other underrepresented populations can get overlooked.

Narrowly defined program areas that may be focused and specialized might not reflect the reality of how certain populations experience their existence. Defined programs with highly specific shorter-term grants create a sense of certainty. In the long run, there is uncertainty. In multi-issue programming, there is less certainty as well. Funding networks beyond single organizations is very complex. The actions of some of the profiled foundations brings both risk and uncertainty. But these foundations embrace both ideas to varying degrees. The very act of listening to communities is an acknowledgement that foundations don't have all of the answers. There is a certain humility that comes from this recognition. Many of the approaches taken by these foundations require some comfort level with risk and uncertainty.

Transcending Grantmaking

Another interesting commonality among these foundations is their willingness to use multiple forms of capital to achieve their ends. They are employing *Passing Gear* philanthropy. *Passing Gear* philanthropy helps foundations transcend various traditional limitations in philanthropic practice.[2] This approach has encouraged foundations to find ways to advance progress through unconventional methods, and apply their capital comprehensively beyond finances. In this sense, foundations are not only grant makers; they are broader civic actors using a range of forms of capital, such as social, moral, intellectual, reputational along with financial.

The approach also challenges foundations to imagine an ideal future beyond existing conditions. The idea of a motivational vision of a brighter future to which foundations can aspire is an important feature in *Passing Gear* philanthropy. Elements of this approach are evident in the profiled foundations. First of all, they are working toward ambitious visions for an improved future for communities, but also for themselves as institutions. They are parting with tradition where necessary, and using other forms of capital beyond grants. These foundations have positioned themselves as civic actors. They are engaging in communities directly, rather than from a distance, and actively seeking to be partners. The nature of their engagement is not only making grants. It is also leveraging funding from other sources, building partnerships, organizing networks, and using program-related investments.

Recognizing the Journey

Many of the profiled foundations reference a "journey". They recognize that they are works in progress as they seek to be more equitable and inclusive. As conversations in philanthropy about DEI continue to evolve, it is increasingly clear that a foundation seeking to become more diverse, equitable, and inclusive evolves at various stages. Some are at earlier stages, and others might be more advanced. Understanding about the characteristics of these phases is evolving as well. A recent study by Equity in the Center identified stages of development for foundations regarding racial equity in particular.[3]

They identified three phases to demonstrate levels of development from "Awake" to "Woke". While their framework focuses specifically on "race equity", it is relevant to the evolution of foundations seeking to achieve some significant level of cultural transformation. The first phase they identified, *Awake* focuses particularly on representation – becoming more racially diverse. The second phase, *Work* involves actively addressing systemic racism and root causes of inequity externally and internally. The third phase, *Woke* is more of a cultural transformation in which organizations are valuing everyone's contributions.[4]

This framework is certainly relevant to the profiled foundations in this book. Whether or not they are emphasizing race on their pathway to cultural change, they are seeking, to varying degrees, some form of cultural change. The process underway at the Meyer Memorial Trust, for example, very much reflects this particular cycle of development. It focused on its composition and began instituting new policies and practices, and is acknowledging it is on a journey to cultural change. What is interesting about this kind of an organizational change process is that there is not necessarily a hard stop once institutional culture has changed. Work would have to continue to progress to assess and renew a cultural commitment. And, very likely, the journey is not linear. People could change, as they often do in organizations, which could alter the flow of progress. There is such variation among foundations. One can certainly observe commonalities in organizational processes. But there are many mitigating circumstances given a foundation's type, history, location, and other factors.

What We Can Learn from These Foundations

These foundations have been challenging themselves as they have been evolving. Many foundations are wondering about appropriate ways in which they can evolve to become more responsive to community needs. It seems there is much to learn from the six foundations profiled for this book.

a   Strengthened lines of communication with constituents can strengthen a foundation strategy's relevance and timeliness.
b   Deepened external engagement seeking to genuinely integrate constituents' perspectives into philanthropic strategy requires change in foundations' institutional practice.
c   Bringing greater representation of constituent populations inside of foundations will likely have an impact on foundation policy, practice, and culture, especially if new voices are fully included.
d   Some aspects of foundation norms should be reviewed honestly and courageously in order to determine where policies and practices might be revised.
e   The needs facing many communities are multiple, intersecting, and complex.
f   Therefore, if foundations want to help communities most adversely impacted by today's most pressing concerns, they should embrace complexity.
g   The process of changing foundations comprehensively to reflect values related to equity and inclusion is lengthy and a departure from existing traditions in philanthropy.
h   The range of ways in which constituents can play a role shaping foundation strategy is vast from opening up dialogue in neighborhoods to creating entirely new philanthropic entities by and for a particular constituency.

This blend of different types of foundations have in common a commitment to changing, and becoming more responsive to the communities they hope to serve. Their approaches vary; and they have different points of emphasis. Their collective efforts are important, as they are attempting to better inform how they organize and channel capital to bring about more equitable outcomes. Their frameworks and techniques provide some guidance about the various tactics foundations can pursue when they want to be more inclusive of stakeholder perspectives and provide particular attention to vulnerable communities that are most adversely affected by the issues they are designed to address.

Notes

1   (The California Endowment 2017)
2   (Hart 2017)
3   (Equity in the Center 2018)
4   Ibid., p. 2.

References

Equity in the Center. *Awake to Woke to Work: Building a Race Equity Culture.* Report of a Project of ProInspire. 2018. https://static1.squarespace.com/static/56b910ccb6aa 60c971d5f98a/t/5adf3de1352f530132863c37/1524579817415/ProInspire-Equity-in-Ce nter-publication.pdf (accessed March 20, 2019).

Hart, Richard. *Philanthropy as the South's Passing Gear: Fulfilling the Promise.* 2017. http://stateofthesouth.org/2017/11/16/philanthropy-as-the-souths-passing-gear-fulfil ling-the-promise/ (accessed March 20, 2019).

The California Endowment. *Diversity, Equity and Inclusion - Audit Report.* 2017. https:// s26107.pcdn.co/wp-content/uploads/TCE-2016-DEI-Audit-Full-Report_Final_Dec-18. pdf (accessed April 20, 2019).

9

CONCLUSIONS

The Nonprofit Sector, Philanthropy, and Society

As we consider the role of philanthropy in society, it is important to recognize the role of the nonprofit sector in society. The nonprofit sector emerged in order to represent, meet the needs of, and strengthen the voice of civil society. In the United States, we think of organizations representing civil society as incorporated organizations. Foundations in the U.S. contribute to organizations with the tax code status, 501c3, which was created out of the 1969 Tax Reform Act. The concept of nonprofit organizations or some form of a third sector beyond the public and private sectors dates back many generations ago.[1] For example, the 1787 Constitutional Convention developed organizations to manage public will.[2]

In some ways, the nonprofit sector has fulfilled this promise, at it has grown and become more institutionalized. In some ways it has not. Indeed, many nonprofit organizations are providing services that fill voids left by government. However, the nongovernmental sector is meant to transcend mere service provision. The sector is not merely an extension or replacement of government. We have a third sector for a reason. This sector represents civil society in a way that can hold the private sector and government accountable. Alexis de Tocqueville, in the 1800s, famously observed democratic behavior in the United States, and recognized an independent spirit, which came with a tendency to create associations.[3] He also expressed concerns about democracies in which a majority could become dominant and wield state power in a manner that suppresses perspectives and influence in civil society.[4]

A healthy nonprofit sector is poised to, not only fill voids left by government, but also to represent civil society and bolster civic participation in the general public. One example of an area that needs far greater attention from the nonprofit sector is voter participation. In democratic contexts in particular, an informed and engaged electorate is crucial to a functioning and effective society. In the United States, for example, voter participation rates are strikingly low. According to the United States Elections Project,[5] in 2016 the United States VEP (voting-eligible population) turnout rates for the presidential election was 60.1%, which had slightly increased from 58.6% in 2012. The November 2018 election is widely recognized for its high voter turnout for all voting age and major racial and ethnic groups.[6] The VEP turnout rate dramatically increased from 36.7% in 2014 to 50.3% in 2018 (data in 2018 is estimated by United States Elections Project[7]).

Presidential elections, as in 2012 and 2016 are the highest rates. Even in these instances, roughly 40% of the population does not vote. In midterm years, such as 2014 and 2018, a solid half of the population does not vote. In democratic societies, voter participation is an expression of the voice of civil society. Society cannot count on the government alone to expand voter participation. This is an area in which the nonprofit sector can play a significant role.

If the nonprofit sector can be a relevant actor in increasing voter participation rates, then philanthropy can play a role in supporting the organizations and efforts that are working in this area. Private philanthropy has been essential to the development of the nonprofit sector. But philanthropy can be more targeted in helping the nonprofit sector fulfill its promise. Moreover, administrations in government come and go. Additionally, governments can be corrupted. Simply replacing philanthropy with government would reduce the capacity of an independent sector. An independent nonprofit sector is positioned to step in when necessary to hold government and the private sector accountable.

With higher voter turnout, one might assume government more accurately reflects the interests of civil society, and feels more accountable. But once administrations are in office, who can hold elected officials accountable? The political engagement of civil society is continuous. Nonprofit advocacy organizations or community organizers, in this regard, can play a particular role. These are the kinds of organizations that can continually highlight where policy makers can do better and champion policies that are working well, particularly for vulnerable populations. As philanthropy possesses capital that can strengthen organizations animating the voices of civil society, foundations can play an especially valuable role.

Philanthropy can be manipulated to enable disproportionate power for wealthy individuals or institutions. Without some measure of accountability for how philanthropic dollars are spent, the idea of philanthropy can move in the opposite direction of representing civil society. This is true in politics where private contributions can be used to bolster particular interests. This is why dialogue about the role of big money in politics continues to be robust, and why some political candidates are increasingly turning to building their base of financial support from grassroots constituencies making small contributions. In any instance, substantial donations can give disproportionate influence to a few wealthy and powerful individuals. Therefore, some conscious effort is required in order to ensure that the interests of large donors do not entirely drive initiatives intended to address crucial societal needs.

As philanthropy continues to grow and evolve, we must wonder about the alignment between societal needs and philanthropic dollars. They don't align automatically. Philanthropy can be better in tune with society when greater lines of communication are established between foundations and the communities they intend to serve, and when foundations are willing to enable the voices of those communities to help shape their priorities. When formations, whether they are incorporated nonprofit organizations or unincorporated associations, adequately represent constituencies, deepened partnership with foundations can be a powerful combination.

Creating Philanthropy's Responsibility to Society

Foundations and philanthropists have choices. Their policies and practices reflect these options as well as their priorities and values. The research for this book set out to gain a better understanding of how foundations can become more responsive to societal needs. While foundations and philanthropists might be regulated in different capacities in the U.S. and other parts of the world, they have quite a bit of flexibility in how they go about making contributions and engaging the constituents they serve. As foundations and donors become more intentional about where they contribute and pay greater attention to how they measure impact, there is a role to play for constituents.

The foundations featured in this book are intentionally expanding their levels of engagement with the constituent communities they intend to serve. Not only do these foundations view these practices as improving their lines of communications with grantees and grantee constituent communities, they see them as vital to the overall strategic intentions of their institutions. They see these practices as fundamental to their missions and purposes. And in the long run, they expect these inclusive approaches to be vital to improving their ultimate impact. They anticipate better results from their deliberate efforts to engage communities. To varying degrees, they also recognize that the values that inform their external engagement should also be reflected in their internal operations and practices. This is not only a matter of greater participation of constituents on the outside of foundations. These featured foundations are continually considering how they model behaviors – systems, policies, practices – inside to reflect the values they are demonstrating outside.

The survival of these foundations is not dependent upon being engaged in communities and inclusive of diverse constituents. This is particularly true for well-endowed foundations. Foundations can choose to avoid engagement, and decide to make all decisions internally and dismiss external input. In many ways, foundations and philanthropists have been able to function and thrive without being diverse, equitable, inclusive, or particularly responsible. Many larger donors have been congratulated for their generosity regardless of their interest in hearing from low income communities. The foundations profiled in this book demonstrate the will to change. They are actively creating a greater degree of responsibility to the communities they hope to improve. They are holding themselves accountable to including the voices of external constitutions and, to varying degrees, allowing these voices to influence their strategic priorities. They are strengthening bridges between philanthropy and society. They are steering away from one-way bridges in which foundations drive all of the decisions and authority and grantees either fall in line or abandon hope of receiving funding. They are building the lines of two-way communication and exchange that can inform strategy.

No, these foundations have not dismantled all power dynamics in philanthropy. It would be naïve to suggest all power dynamics between foundations and constituents will diminish. The LankellyChase Foundation is questioning its very being as a foundation in continuous recognition of the inherent power dynamics attached to merely being a philanthropic institution. But they are taking steps to limit their dominance in relating to the communities they serve. As a community foundation, the San Francisco Foundation chose to pursue a strategy emphasizing equity based on what they heard from their listening sessions in various neighborhoods in their region. While many community foundations are focused more on the interests of their donors, the San Francisco Foundation made a decision to first hear from residents in neighborhoods. It then determined to develop a strategy based on equity because this is what the foundation heard from communities. The foundation's discussions with donors came afterward. It asked its donors to consider its equity-focused strategy in its contributions. In this instance, a community foundation decided to prioritize the perspectives of residents in its region as a means of developing a philanthropic strategy. These were inclusively strategic in this regard.

The question of choice is very significant in these instances. When we ask what is the responsibility of philanthropy to society, we could say it is to address important societal needs that are not otherwise being served. But how can anyone ensure that the decisions of foundations are being influenced by the needs of a population a foundation emphasizes? It is very difficult to determine if any systems are in place to determine the degree of a foundation's responsiveness to society. Therefore, particular foundations have to create them. The Mary Reynolds Babcock Foundation recognized that it had to build in a greater physical presence in the various communities it serves in order to have a greater impact. The foundation realized that, as a family foundation, it could be more responsive as an institution if it included constituents from Southern communities among the family members on the Board of Directors. These are choices. Whether or not the foundation is mandated by some public order to be responsive and in tune with societal priorities, the foundations profiled in this book decided that is their responsibility to be more inclusive.

Greater Awareness in Philanthropy

The National Committee on Responsive Philanthropy[8] (NCRP) has been a true trailblazer on matters of the responsibility of philanthropy to society. NCRP "promotes philanthropy that serves the public good, is responsive to people and communities with the least wealth and opportunity, and is held accountable to the highest standards of integrity and openness."[9] NCRP conducts research and produces reports. Much of their work highlights how foundations are going about being responsive to the needs of underrepresented communities and challenging philanthropic practice that is not. They connect to foundations, and hope to increase the use of their tools and resources in philanthropy. They expect this increased understanding of the role that foundations can play particularly in supporting organizations involved in existing movements for social change. In the long run, they hope to increase giving to social justice and underrepresented communities. They promote long-term general support funding for social justice.[10]

NCRP is a member of Change Philanthropy,[11] which is a coalition of ten organizations that champion various aspects of diversity, equity, and inclusion in philanthropy. This organization periodically holds a significance conference, the Unity Summit, which focuses on a variety of ways in which philanthropy can become more responsible and accountable to diverse constituents. Among members of Change Philanthropy are the Association of Black Foundation Executives, Native Americans in Philanthropy, Hispanics in Philanthropy, and Asian Americans and Pacific Islanders in Philanthropy. These are organizations in the philanthropic field that represent communities of color. These organizations have played a crucial role in getting philanthropy as a field to include communities of color within their institutions and in their external engagement. While many of the issues foundations address – health, education, etc. – are most adversely affecting communities of color, foundations are notoriously not particularly diverse themselves.[12] And, as demographic data collection on grantees continues to grow, it is becoming increasingly clear that the organizations that receive the vast majority of funds in the U.S. are not led by people of color.

Overall, the philanthropic field in the United States has become more of an identifiable industry including numerous associations and professionals. The number of Philanthropy Serving Organizations (PSOs) has continued to proliferate. The membership association that brings together PSOs in the United States – the United Philanthropy Forum[13] – has experienced steady growth over the last few years. This organization brings together associations focusing on particular regions in the U.S., those that focus on specific issue areas, and those that focus on specific population groups. The Forum has been increasingly emphasizing the importance of foundations engaging communities and being responsive to community needs, particularly through the lens of racial equity. The Forum's Racial Equity Committee helps the Forum determine how to prioritize racial equity in its own organization and enhance its capacity to help its members communicate with their foundation members about how to address racial inequities and be more inclusive of communities of color in their work.

The philanthropic field outside of the United States is growing as well. The Network of European Foundations brings together leading European foundations promoting philanthropic cooperation around social inclusion, international development and democracy.[14] WINGS (Worldwide Initiatives for Grantmaker Support) is a network of over 130 organizations representing 45 countries promoting the development of philanthropy and social investment.[15] This association focuses on the organizations supporting philanthropy – the Philanthropy Serving Organizations. They are leveraging the role of these organizations to connect globally around the role that philanthropy can play in civil society. WINGS emphasizes systems change and explicitly addresses "power imbalances".[16] They are leveraging an "ecosystem" of organizations supporting philanthropy to collaborate globally.

The evolution of this organization is an interesting development. It not only demonstrates the further institutionalization of a global philanthropic field, but it is stressing the areas in which traditional philanthropy is being increasingly challenged. The profiled foundations in this book are grappling with breaking from tradition in their singular institutions, but there is evidence that an organized field of philanthropy is not only growing, but highlighting limitations and seeking to catalyze new directions. WINGS is also explicit about the role of philanthropy in civil society, and the importance of philanthropy's contributions in diverse democracies.

In the United States in particular, the awareness of the importance of responsive and inclusive philanthropy has been gradually growing. There has probably never been a time in which there has been more discussion about racial equity, equity in general, diversity, and inclusion in philanthropy. As foundation funding[17] focused on improving foundation's commitment to these concerns increases, discussions and initiatives will only continue.

Discussions about how to make foundations more accountable and responsive to societal needs and underserved communities have been very apparent in an expanded body of literature on philanthropy as well.

First of all, criticism of philanthropy has grown sharper in some recent books. In *Winners Take All*, Anand Giridharadas highlights how a global elite preserves the status quo through philanthropy. In his view, the wealthy, under the guise of seeking to improve the world, mask their own role in causing and maintaining inequities.[18] Robert Reich, in *Just Giving*, argues that the apparent generosity of the wealthy can actually undermine democratic values. Larger scale philanthropy in particular, according to Reich, is an exercise in power to influence the public without much accountability.[19] Edgar Villanueva, in *Decolonizing Wealth* emphasizes the colonial dimensions manifested in philanthropy.[20] He maintains that philanthropy mirrors the hierarchical dimensions of colonialism despite a façade suggesting otherwise.

The chorus of arguments against the entrenched power dynamics in philanthropy is growing louder. But in the midst of the very necessary voices that clarify our understanding of the true nature of philanthropy, and its limitations, there are efforts underway within philanthropy to counter, on some level, clear shortcomings in this field of work. The intent of this book is to highlight some ways in which particular foundations are attempting to counter traditional power dynamics in philanthropy in hopes that examples can be instructive to others. Indeed, there is much work to be done; and no foundation is perfect in its ability to dismantle the power and contradictions inherent in philanthropy. At the very least, there are people in philanthropy who are willing to raise the issues. Someone such as Villanueva, for example, is in philanthropy and working at a foundation. Having been in and around philanthropy for over a couple of decades myself, I can see that awareness of how to make philanthropy more equitable, just, inclusive, and responsive to community needs has increased. The challenge is to both expand the level of awareness as well as to manifest ideas about how philanthropy can transform into practice.

From Awareness to Practice

This book focuses on how specific foundations are developing policies and practices to become more inclusive to illustrate how values and principles are manifested in practice. Dialogue is very important in advancing change in philanthropy as well as other fields. However, ideas do not become tangible reality until they are actually tested. It is one thing to declare that foundations should be more accountable, it is another to demonstrate what it takes for a foundation to be diverse, equitable, and inclusive in practice. There is certainly a desire among an increased number of foundations to understand what it would mean to be more engaged with constituent populations, particularly those that would stand the most to gain from equitable education, for example. Foundations are increasingly inquiring about racial equity in particular. As a recent study[21] for the United Philanthropy Forum indicated, the visibility of incidents of racism (i.e. police brutality), the climate around the 2016 U.S. elections, and the increased dialogue in philanthropy about diversity have pushed many PSOs to explore how to create programming on racial equity for their member foundations.

My company, Marga Incorporated, has been coordinating the work of the Race and Equity in Philanthropy Group (REPG)[22] since 2006. This effort brings together a growing cluster of foundations to discuss specific policies and practices. A range of different types of foundations are participating members in this group: The Annie E. Casey Foundation, The California Endowment, The California Wellness Foundation, The East Bay Community Foundation, The Ford Foundation, The James Irvine Foundation, The Jacob and Valeria Langeloth Foundation, The Lumina Foundation, The San Francisco Foundation, The Winthrop Rockefeller Foundation, and the W.K. Kellogg Foundation. In many ways, this group inspired this book for a couple of reasons. First of all, the group focuses specifically on policies and practices for the entire foundation. It addresses foundations systemically, and emphasizes how specifically foundations can become more diverse, equitable, and inclusive. Secondly, the group includes a mix of varying types of foundations. The philanthropic field is comprised of a range of types of foundations – family foundations, community foundations, etc. These dynamics, as illustrated throughout this book, are fairly significant in our understanding of how a foundation can embrace certain values and then put them into practice.

As philanthropy continues to evolve, it will be increasingly important to be able to demonstrate actual change in policies and practices in specific foundations. The foundations profiled in this book have developed particular ways to build and expand lines of communication with grantees and grantee constituent communities in order to influence strategic priorities. This is one dimension of the broader discussion about DEI. It is a very important one because it challenges the fundamental way in which foundations tend to do business. Foundations are often considered to be insular, even impenetrable, to certain populations. In the nonprofit sector, the power dynamic places foundations in one position, separate and apart from the organizations that require philanthropic support in order to fulfill their missions. Grantees are challenged to both represent the communities they serve as well as break down the barriers to foundations, and secure funding. Often, smaller nonprofit organizations, which very well may be highly representative of their communities are unable to penetrate foundations. The more well-connected, often white-led, larger nonprofits are often better positioned with foundations and philanthropists. When taking account of the unique dynamics of wealth, those possessing greater wealth have access to other persons with wealth. Therefore, there are built in advantages for those nonprofits that are led by well-connected individuals.

With these established dynamics in philanthropy, it is important that particular foundations set themselves apart and demonstrate what can be done to change the dynamics by example. A foundation setting a different pace has a particular significance. REPG is predicated upon the importance of peer learning as an avenue to change in philanthropy. As philanthropy tends to be an insulated field, foundations learn well from peers – other foundations. REPG meetings are learning exchanges in which foundation representatives hear of each other's practices related to racial equity and inclusion. When one foundation representative hears how another foundation has, for example, enhanced how it retrieves input from local communities, it is easier for that one person to influence her/his foundation to consider a similar practice. Since foundations come in so many shapes and sizes, it is useful to be able to know how inclusive practices are manifested in different types of foundations.

Expanding the Scale of Inclusive Practice

This multiplier effect of leveraging the policies and practices of one foundation, by example, to influence others is one way to expand the number of strategically inclusive foundations. When a larger critical mass of foundations are employing the kinds of approaches explored by the six foundations featured herein, the philanthropic field is moving closer to transformation. It is important to explore practices at the level of individual foundations, but also at the fieldwide level in philanthropy as well. Consequently, it is important to share stories and lessons from particular foundations that have begun to transform how they interface with their constituents.

Directions for Philanthropy

Institutional mission is a significant aspect of the future direction of inclusion as a central aspect of how foundations develop and implement their strategic priorities. Foundations have social missions. They are tax-exempt entities with some built in expectation to fulfill a public purpose. However, as mentioned, foundations do not automatically transcend convention and take extra steps to ensure connection and responsiveness to constituent communities. In many ways, the concept of strategic philanthropy has suggested the opposite – foundations close ranks, set priorities, and find ways to fit nonprofits into the decisions that have already been firmly entrenched.

It should not be a stretch to suggest foundations expand their engagement with communities, or make their policies and practices more inclusive and equitable. These ideas are consistent with a social mission. Strategy in the corporate world is a question of differentiation among competitors in order to increase market share. While some dimension of competitiveness along these lines exists in the nonprofit sector, organizations with social missions have different considerations. Organizations with social missions have to consider a set of values differently because their intended goals are based on some form of societal enhancement, whereas the drive around corporate strategy is to maximize profits. If the drive for foundations is to maximize societal benefit, what should a foundation take into account? It would seem that a crucial component of developing a foundation's strategic imperative would be the active participation of grantees and grantee constituent communities.

Making the case to foundations to become more engaged, responsive, and inclusive should not be difficult. However, this paradigm is unconventional in philanthropy. Philanthropy is rooted in the power of wealth. It is an extension of wealth created through the profit motive, and it carries the established dimensions of inequality. Therefore, there is some work to be done to change the mindset that is typically embedded in philanthropy, particularly with respect to power. Philanthropy will have to take a closer self-critical look at itself as a field. And each foundation will have to continue asking whether it is doing enough. But, as noted, building from examples is one potential path to helping foundations deepen their commitment to the communities that could benefit the most from their efforts. Here are some suggested ways in which foundations can become more inclusively strategic:

- *Learn from other foundations that have transcended*
  This is the premise of this book – that we can draw lessons from foundations that have challenged themselves to change, and developed new
  methods, policies, and practices. We have enough of a critical mass of
  foundations that have experiences and lessons to share, including those
  profiled in this book and those participating in communities of practice,
  such as the Race and Equity in Philanthropy Group.
- *Review mission and purpose and consider community impact*
  If a foundation has not had much experience taking a more equitable and
  inclusive approach to its philanthropy and practice, then it is best to first
  assess the situation. Is the foundation making much of an impact at the
  community level? Are the foundation's funds reaching the populations
  most adversely impacted by the issues the foundation intends to address? Is
  the mission of the foundation timely and relevant given the priority needs
  of this time?
- *Self-educate about equity and inclusion*
  As examples of foundations that have ventured toward a more equitable
  and inclusive approach have increased, there is a growing body of publications, tools, and resources on these issues, and how they relate to philanthropy. Foundations can bring in speakers with expertise in these areas,
  read and hold discussions, visit other foundations with a track record on
  equity and inclusion, attend conferences, listen to webinars, and pursue
  many other forms of education.
- *Broaden the foundation's networks*
  Philanthropy has a tendency to be insular and highly dependent upon
  trusted relationships. Many grants and other opportunities emerge through
  foundations' existing networks. At times, these networks can be particularly elite, and not necessarily connected to underrepresented, underserved, and vulnerable communities. But there are always existing
  associations and organizations representing these communities that are not
  necessarily connected to foundations. Courageous foundations reach out
  to new networks and open new lines of communication.
- *Increase time in places and deepen communication with constituents*
  Similarly, it is difficult to be accurately in tune with the needs of communities without spending time in them. As the experiences of foundations profiled in this book demonstrate, visiting and listening to
  communities can reshape and improve philanthropic strategies. Moreover,
  focusing on places can help sharpen foundations' ability to, not only
  deepen relationships with community-based constituents, but develop
  focused strategy to address crucial issues as they are manifested in places. As
  foundations pursue measurable results, focus on defined places clarifies goal
  setting and enables greater partnership between foundations and community-based constituents.

- *Embrace long-term commitments and risk*

  The continuous pursuit of short-term results typically underestimates the complexities of issues facing communities. The pathways of a grant period, even one as short as a single year, are often not linear. What is often proposed ends up evolving through trial and error. The most challenging issues are typically not resolved in a year or even a few years. Some foundations fear long-term commitment, perhaps concerned that things will go wrong. Well, they probably will go wrong in some capacity over several years because improving education outcomes or reducing health disparities are hard.

- *Revising thinking on evaluation and learning*

  One reason these issues are hard to address is the multivariate nature of the problems themselves as well as the solutions. We have seen the rise of understanding about social determinants of health, for example. Health outcomes are influenced by income, housing, schooling, location, the environment, etc. Therefore, the strategies to seek improvements in population health appropriately must be multifaceted. These strategies don't lend themselves to quickly measurable quantitative outcomes. Along the path of longer term strategies, comes a great deal of learning – learning which may not have been anticipated at all in existing evaluation frameworks.

- *Explore investments in networks of organizations*

  If the issues and strategies are multifaceted, then numerous different stakeholders are required to participate in finding solutions. Some of the foundations profiled in this book come to this conclusion, as they have gone into places, listened to constituents, learned of the complexity of issues in these places, and invested in networks working on various levels over longer term time horizons. Every community is an ecosystem of people and organizations that have a stake. Foundations should be willing to work to understand these systems and collaborate with local constituents.

- *Expand investments to organizations led by and serving underrepresented communities*

  Many recent critical discussions on philanthropy have challenged the limited resources to organizations that are actually representing the communities that are most impacted by inequities. These are often organizations that have smaller budgets and are considered to have limited capacity. But they often have tremendous assets because they are representative of their communities. They may not be incorporated at all. But these organizations can play a crucial role in solving the most pressing issues facing communities.

- *Support capacity building of grassroots organizations*

  Organizations that are led by and serving their communities at the grassroots level might not have sophisticated systems or much money at all. But they may do a great deal on a small budget. While some foundations will merely avoid investing in smaller organizations, they could play a role in helping them to grow and develop. Technical assistance and capacity building can help strengthen these organizations. Foundations can work with technical assistance providers or even build their internal capability to assist these organizations.

- *Leverage Board and staff composition to bring lived experiences inside*
  As demonstrated in the experiences of some of the profiled foundations, the composition of who is doing the work in philanthropy matters. People who represent the populations foundations hope to impact or improve have an intimate understanding of their experiences. People who have experience working to address the issues the foundation prioritize also bring unique insights that can strengthen a foundation's strategic direction. The foundations featured in this book bring instructive lessons about the value and impact of diversifying Boards and staffs. This changed composition better positions foundations to be inclusive and equitable in their work.

- *Challenge grantees that are not representative to change*
  Finally, nonprofit organizations that receive support from foundations are not always representative of their communities. They often have not been challenged by foundations to do otherwise. There is growing interest and effort to collect demographic data on grantees to understand the levels of diversity or representation of grantee organizations. Foundations are beginning to require this data collection of organizations that are applying for grants. This illustrates the influential role that foundations can play in encouraging nonprofit organizations to be more diverse, equitable, and inclusive.

Fieldwide, philanthropy has much room for further reflection and exploration.

- *Leverage associations of foundations for great impact*
  Individual foundations, as noted, can transform and alter their policies, methods, and practices. But the field of philanthropy continues to grow. The number of Philanthropy Serving Organizations continues to proliferate. These associations each reach multiple foundations. Behavior change to a greater scale can be leveraged through organizations such as the United Philanthropy Forum, which is an association of these PSOs. The numerous other aforementioned associations all have a role to play in setting the tone or providing levels of education and guidance to their member foundations.

- *Highlight and disseminate case examples of foundations that have transcended*
  As foundations learn from foundations, it is always useful to highlight specific case examples of philanthropic institutions that have become more equitable and inclusive, and have drawn the connection between how they relate to constituent populations and their overall strategic priorities. The transformation of a foundation's thinking and practice, as noted, is more of a journey than an instantaneous transition. Foundations should understand the intricacies of how institutions grapple with change, achieve successes and confront challenges. Foundations should understand what it

takes to transform into a more equitable and inclusive institution that is fundamentally strategic. It is important to capture and disseminate the lessons and experiences of foundations that have undergone such evolutions.

- *Expand the cadre of individuals in philanthropy who are committed to equity and inclusion*

  The philanthropic field should also play a role in expanding the number of people inside and outside of foundations committed to these issues. Fellows and leadership development programs that are intentional in this regard can be very useful. As the experiences of foundations featured in this book demonstrate, individuals can make a considerable difference in catalyzing institutional transformation. Someone has to start the conversation and hold the foundation accountable to going further. Sometimes a CEO or the Board can lead this charge, but people at varying levels in foundations can be pivotal as well. The more people who are committed to these principles, the more likely foundations will change and evolve.

- *Facilitate the development of many more indigenous foundations by and for constituent populations*

  The reality of many philanthropic institutions is that people of some wealth tend to start foundations. The case of TrustAfrica demonstrates an example of a foundation that is by and for Africans. This type of foundation is an important illustration of how to turn philanthropy over to the very populations thought to be the recipients rather than the donors. TrustAfrica is also becoming a vehicle to continually build African philanthropy, pooling resources from African donors in addition to their funding from the Ford Foundation. As we think of many other constituencies that could benefit from foundations explicitly representing their interests, perhaps multiple philanthropists could combine resources to create more of these entirely representative philanthropic institutions. As previously noted, the W.K. Kellogg Foundation's Catalyzing Community Giving program is one example of a foundation initiative designed to strengthen this kind of community philanthropy.

- *Creating spaces for peer learning*

  The Race and Equity in Philanthropy Group (REPG) has maintained a space for peer learning among foundations from across the United States for several years. This peer learning has helped representatives of member foundations bring particular ideas for policies and practices that have been discussed in meetings back to their institutions. This model has continued to influence institutional change paired with peer support. This forum has helped foundations support each other through the journey of institutional change. This group is now in the process of expanding the number of peer learning spaces by working with PSOs and clusters of their members. Through this kind of dialogue and exchange, we can create more examples of foundations with a demonstrable track record and specific policies and practices that can model behavior for other foundations. When a foundation can point to a set of practices at a peer institution, change can be accelerated. Seeing that another foundation has tried and succeeded reduces the perception of risk and helps foundations make the case for change internally. This group started because the Annie E. Casey Foundation wanted to learn from other foundations dating back to 2002. I was asked to interview foundations on their behalf to facilitate their learning. But the interviewees wanted to learn as well. So, we started coordinating focus groups that evolved into a permanent table for learning exchange and collective improvement. With more of these kinds of communities of practice among foundations seeking to be more equitable and inclusive, we should have more foundations that have improved policies and practices. These changes should lead to improvements in communities and greater change in philanthropy as well.

Overall, this is an important moment in philanthropy. There is now enough of a critical mass of people in philanthropy wanting to see change. We also have more specific foundations that have undergone some degree of transformation, such as those profiled in this book. There is a great deal from which to build. Being able to highlight the work of particular foundations helps us move from rhetoric to reality. In a time when philanthropy is facing increased criticism, we have to be able to show what philanthropy can do when there is a commitment to equity and inclusion. And this commitment does not make foundations less strategic. At the very least, it grounds them in reality, which could only mean equitable and inclusive foundations are more strategic.

The foundations profiled in this book are inspirational in addition to being instructive. The pathway that led to their changes was stimulated by candid self-assessments and a willingness to break with tradition. The universe of foundations is as wide-ranging (even more so) as the foundations in these pages. If we are to understand such a complex field, we have to explore the particular experiences and cultures of foundations of varying types. And yet, we can see commonalities across these six very different institutions. They are works in progress, as are all foundations. But they are, in different ways, envisioning a more equitable and inclusive future. If philanthropy is to reach its potential as an agent of change and overall improvement in society, we will need particular foundations that are willing to transform, and we will want to learn how their experiences can reframe and reorient philanthropy as a whole.

Notes

1 (Muslic 2017)
2 Ibid.
3 (Tocqueville 1961)
4 (Cohen 2006)
5 Ibid.

6 (United States Census Bureau 2019)
7 (United States Elections Project 2019)
8 (National Committee for Responsive Philanthropy, *Homepage*, 2019)
9 (National Committee for Responsive Philanthropy, *About Us*, 2019)
10 (National Committee for Responsive Philanthropy, *About Us – Strategic Framework*, 2019)
11 (Change Philanthropy, *Homepage*, 2019)
12 (The Diversity 5 Coalition 2016)
13 (United Philanthropy Forum, *Homepage*, 2019)
14 (The Network of European Foundations, *Homepage*, 2019)
15 (Worldwide Initiatives for Grantmaker Support, *Homepage*, 2019)
16 (Worldwide Initiatives for Grantmaker Support, *About WINGS*, 2019)
17 One important example is the funding that the Ford Foundation and the W.K. Kellogg Foundation have invested in Borealis Philanthropy's Racial Equity Fund, which "is to promote grantmaking strategies that promote structural change and ending racial disparities as the norm in philanthropy" (Borealis Philanthropy 2019).
18 (Giridharadas 2018)
19 (Reich 2018)
20 (Villanueva 2018)
21 (United Philanthropy Forum 2018)
22 (Marga Inc. 2019)

References

Borealis Philanthropy. *Racial Equity in Philanthropy Fund*. 2019. https://borealisphilanthropy.org/grantmaking/racial-equity-in-philanthropy-fund/

Change Philanthropy. *Homepage*. 2019. www.changephilanthropy.org (accessed August 8, 2019).

Cohen, Adam. Democracy in America, then and now, a struggle against majority tyranny. *The New York Times*. 2006. https://www.nytimes.com/2006/01/23/opinion/democracy-in-america-then-and-now-a-struggle-against-majority.html (accessed May 10, 2019).

Giridharadas, Anand. *Winners Take All: The Elite Charade of Changing the World*. Knopf, 2018.

Marga Inc. *Race and Equity in Philanthropy Group (REPG)*. 2019. https://www.margainc.com/repg/ (accessed August 2, 2019).

Muslic, Hannah. *A Brief History of Nonprofit Organizations (And What We Can Learn)*. 2017. https://nonprofithub.org/starting-a-nonprofit/a-brief-history-of-nonprofit-organizations/ (accessed May 10, 2019).

National Committee for Responsive Philanthropy. *About Us – Strategic Framework*. 2019. https://www.ncrp.org/about-us/strategic-framework/strategic-framework-infographic (accessed August 10, 2019).

National Committee for Responsive Philanthropy. *About Us*. 2019. https://www.ncrp.org/about-us (accessed August 10, 2019).

National Committee for Responsive Philanthropy. *Homepage*. 2019. www.ncrp.org (accessed August 10, 2019).

Reich, Rob. *Just Giving: Why Philanthropy is Failing Democracy and How It Can Do Better*. Princeton University Press, 2018.

The Diversity 5 Coalition. *Stories from the Movement – to Advance Diversity, Equity, and Inclusion*. Fifth in an Annual Series Reports. 2016. http://www.d5coalition.org/wp-content/uploads/2016/04/D5-SOTW-2016-Final-web-pages.pdf (accessed August 8, 2019).

The Network of European Foundations. *Homepage*. 2019. https://www.nef-europe.org/ (accessed August 2, 2019).

Tocqueville, Alexis de. *Democracy in America* [1835] 1961. New York: Schocken. http://xroads.virginia.edu/~HYPER/DETOC/ (accessed May 9, 2019).

United Philanthropy Forum. *Advancing Racial Equity in Philanthropy: A Scan of Philanthropy-Serving Organizations*. 2018. https://www.unitedphilforum.org/racialequityscan (accessed August 2, 2019).

United Philanthropy Forum. *Homepage*. 2019. www.unitedphilforum.org (accessed August 2, 2019).

United States Census Bureau. *Voter Turnout Rates Among All Voting Age and Major Racial and Ethnic Groups Were Higher Than in 2014*. 2019. https://www.census.gov/library/stories/2019/04/behind-2018-united-states-midterm-election-turnout.html (accessed August 10, 2019).

United States Elections Project. *National Turnout Rates*. 2019. http://www.electproject.org/home/voter-turnout/voter-turnout-data (accessed August 10, 2019).

Villanueva, Edgar. *Decolonizing Wealth: Indigenous Wisdom to Heal Divides and Restore Balance*. 1st ed. Oakland, CA: Berrett Koehler Publishers. 2018.

Worldwide Initiatives for Grantmaker Support. *About WINGS*. 2019. https://www.wingsweb.org/page/AboutWINGS (accessed August 2, 2019).

Worldwide Initiatives for Grantmaker Support. *Homepage*. 2019. https://www.wingsweb.org/default.aspx (accessed August 2, 2019).

INDEX

Note: Information in figures is indicated by page numbers in *italics*.